The

South Bank

HAMLET

edited by

R. R. Young, B.A.

Senior English Master, Hertford Grammar School

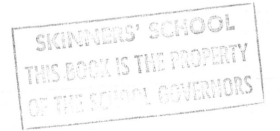

University Tutorial Press

Published by University Tutorial Press Ltd
9-10 Great Sutton Street, London EC1V 0DA

This edition is set in Times New Roman

Published 1965
Reprinted 1970, 1977

ISBN: 0 7231 0533 2

PRINTED AND BOUND BY WEATHERBY WOOLNOUGH,
WELLINGBOROUGH,
NORTHANTS.

PREFATORY NOTE

THIS new edition of the play uses the full text prepared by Professor Peter Alexander,* a text which has found favour with several Examining Boards, both at home and overseas, and has been selected for various G.C.E. Examinations. Present-day students and teachers will doubtless welcome the opportunity for a more mature approach to the play through an unexpurgated text. Similarly, the Notes have been written to take account of modern scholarship, and with the requirements of the modern student in mind. The Introduction offers a critical appraisal of the play, and the annotated Bibliography supplements this in sufficient detail to provide for the university and college student.

Hamlet was almost certainly written in 1601. The text is from the Folio of 1623 which appears to have been printed from a playhouse copy of the Quarto, possibly with Shakespeare's autograph corrections.

R. R. Y.

ACKNOWLEDGMENT

The cover illustration is taken from the central section of Visscher's engraving of 1611. For providing photographs and permission to reproduce it thanks are due to the Trustees of the British Museum.

* From the Shakespeare volumes in Collins Classics with permission of William Collins Sons and Company Ltd, Glasgow.

CONTENTS

INTRODUCTION

Shakespeare's Life.—William Shakespeare was born in 1564 at Stratford-on-Avon in Warwickshire, where his father, John Shakespeare, was in business. Of William between the times of his baptism and of his marriage in his nineteenth year to Anne Hathaway (a woman some eight years his senior) we know nothing, though it is conjectured that he was educated, in the Latin language and literature chiefly, at Stratford Grammar School. Between 1583 and 1585 three children were born to him—Susanna in 1583 and Hamnet and Judith (twins) in 1585.

About this time he must have left Stratford for London (it is possible that a visit of the Queen's Players to Stratford in 1587 was the occasion which prompted his departure). We next hear of him in 1592 when he appears to have aroused the jealousy of Robert Greene, one of a group of "University wits" who wrote for the stage. Greene warns his fellow dramatists of "an upstart crow beautified with our feathers" who "supposes he is as well able to bombast out a blank verse as the best of you; and, being an absolute Johannes Factotum, is in his own conceit the only Shakescene in the country". It is clear that the young "upstart" from Warwickshire had already been too successful to please established writers.

The dedication in 1593 of Shakespeare's first published work, *Venus and Adonis,* shows that he had by that time some associations with men of rank for it is dedicated to the Earl of Southampton, as is also *Lucrece* in the following year; and Southampton is thought to have been of considerable help to the poet. In 1594 we find Shakespeare acting at court as one of the Lord Chamberlain's Men, the theatrical company for which he wrote and acted throughout his career. Some evidence of his growing popularity may be gained from the fact that certain of his plays began to appear in print in 1597, and in that year he was sufficiently prosperous to purchase for

his family New Place, the biggest house in Stratford (though
he himself did not settle permanently there until later in life).
He was now regarded by his contemporaries as their chief
dramatist, able to outshine all "*that insolent* Greece *or
haughtie* Rome *sent forth*", in Ben Jonson's famous words.
He became a partner in the Globe Theatre in 1599, made
further investments at Stratford, and retired there about 1610
or 1611. He died in 1616.

The Plays.—It is customary to group Shakespeare's plays
chronologically into four periods. In the first period (1590-5)
we see Shakespeare serve and pass rapidly out of his appren-
ticeship. He early attempts all three kinds of play: *Titus
Andronicus* is a tragedy of horror of a type very popular at that
time; the three *Henry VI* plays form a trilogy of histories—the
Elizabethans were again very fond of chronicle plays: the
Comedy of Errors is a comedy on a classical theme, possibly
written partly to show that such a play was not the monopoly
of the "university wits". To the second period (1596-1600)
belong the great comedies and histories; and their humour
and zest for living is obviously Shakespeare's; but it also
reflects to some extent the mood of the English people at this
time. By the early years of the seventeenth century, however,
that mood has changed; soon a new monarch ascends the
throne, the golden age is over, and cynicism and disillusionment are to be found everywhere. Shakespeare himself
becomes preoccupied with the irony and tragedy of life, and
this is the stuff of the plays of his third period (1601-8), the
period of the great tragedies, *Hamlet*, *Othello*, *Lear*, and
Macbeth, and of the "dark comedies", so called because in
them, despite a "happy ending", the sense of life's gaiety is
absent, the sense of its nastiness very much present. Nevertheless, if the message of *Hamlet* is that the tragedy of life is
complete, in the beginnings of Lear's regeneration in his
realisation amidst his own suffering of the sufferings of
others, there is a sign that all is not loss. In the plays of the
final period (1609-12) regeneration through suffering and
penitence, leading to reconciliation and peace, has become the

main theme. These last plays, with their large romance and masque elements, were written with the tastes of the court in mind; and reflect the serenity the poet has attained to after the spiritual turmoil of earlier years.

The Theatres.—The theatres at which Shakespeare's plays were performed were of two kinds, "public" and "private".

The public theatres.—In the earlier sixteenth century plays were often performed in the courtyards of inns, with the spectators standing round three sides of a temporary stage at one end, and possibly watching from the windows or balconies. When theatres came to be built in London their designers had this in mind, and thus left their buildings open to the sky, with the stage jutting right out into the audience who were still expected to stand. Round the sides, however, were covered galleries in which seating was provided for those who paid more; the young bloods of means would sometimes hire stools on the sides of the stage itself, and not infrequently made a great nuisance of themselves. The shape of the theatres—square, round, or hexagonal—together with the fact that the stage seems usually to have covered half the total floor space—ensured that no member of the audience was ever more than a few yards away from the actors.

At the back of the main or apron stage was a gallery which was used when scenes set on, for instance, a balcony or castle wall were required. Beneath this was a recess or inner stage (sometimes known as the "Study") across which a curtain could be drawn; it was used for some interior scenes, the hovel in which Lear shelters, for example. The Study was flanked on either side by doors through which the actors might make their entrances. Above the first gallery in some theatres (the Globe was probably one) was another—a musicians'—gallery. It seems likely that these galleries, whether the theatre possessed one or two, were sometimes used to hold spectators if not otherwise required. Above them was a roof (the "Heavens") painted with stars, supported by pillars from the stage and covering only the rear part of it; and above the roof again was a short tower (the "Hut") containing machinery which might lower a "heavenly throne" to the stage. From that tower a flag would be hoisted in the morning if there was to be a performance in the afternoon (there were no evening performances for the players depended on daylight) and a trumpet would be blown when a play was about to commence. Beneath the main stage, out of sight of the audience, was the "Cellarage" from which entrances might be made through a trap door, and probably more than one; a ghost might speak from the Cellarage, and make his appearances and disappearances through the trap door.

No scenery was used in the productions. This does not, however, mean that there was little for the eye of the spectator to delight in. The stage was painted as brightly as a fair, and decorated with tapestries hung from the pillars and elsewhere, gay for comedy, sombre for tragedy. The actors wore rich costumes, often purchased second-hand from the nobility, and there were many scenes of pageantry in which colourful banners were borne. Properties were used—tables, stools, etc., and we know that the Admiral's men had, amongst other items, a rock, a Hell Mouth, Phaeton's chariot, and "Kent's wooden leg" as well as several heads—for "Old Mahomet", Iris, and Argus, for instance. But despite such aids it is clear that Shakespeare's audiences expected to use their imaginations more than their modern counterparts. The Prologue in *Henry V* advised them, "Think when we talk of horses, that you see them", and they were skilled at doing so. When they saw a single branch or possibly a box shrub they knew that a forest was intended; candles or torches meant that it was night.

The producer of to-day, accustomed to a proscenium arch, drop curtain, and all the modern stage resources, none of which the Elizabethans possessed, would, however, be mistaken to feel superior to them. The world's greatest drama was written with their theatres in mind, and no doubt the marvellous richness and evocativeness of the verse of Shakespeare and his fellow playwrights is to some extent due to the necessity of creating atmosphere without help from lighting or décor. The very simplicity of the staging enabled a play to proceed at pace (two hours was usual as against a common two and a half to three and a half hours to-day) with a consequent gain in dramatic effect. One scene ended when the characters walked off, the next began when the others walked on: the one scene might be in Alexandria, the other in Rome, a transition which the later theatre could not obtain without dropping the curtain and changing the scenery (but for which radio and film have a parallel technique in the "fade"). There was an intimacy between actor and audience which is not possible to-day when they are separated by the footlights; and devices such as the soliloquy enabled him to share his thoughts with them as with a close friend.

The private theatres.—Not all dramatic performances took place out of doors. The players had long been accustomed to acting in the houses of noblemen, at the universities of Oxford and Cambridge, and at the Inns of Court, usually on a temporary stage at one end of the great hall. In the later sixteenth century several indoor theatres came into being, open to the public but called private because they were smaller and more exclusive than the others, charged higher prices, and had an atmosphere similar to that of the genuinely private performances just referred to. They were lit by candlelight and this must have been a great help in creating dramatic illusion. Presumably their stages resembled those of the public theatres, though the acting would be more subtle for the actors did not need to declaim their parts as in the open air—the fact that until 1608 only boys' companies used them probably contributed to a quieter style of presentation. In 1608 Shakespeare's company took over the Blackfriars so that they had one private and one public theatre (the Globe); the same actors played at both—it may be that one was used mainly in the winter, the other in summer.

London was the only city which had theatres of either kind. When the companies toured the provinces, as they did particularly in summer to escape the recurring plague in the capital, they still acted in the inn yards or in any other suitable place in the traditional manner.

Court performances.—Elizabeth sometimes, and James I frequently, summoned the players to give performances at court, particularly during the twelve days of Christmas. These performances would take place in the great hall of one of the royal palaces with the stage set at one end, possibly with a painted backcloth. But on the first night of *Twelfth Night*, a play specially written for the court, the stage seems to have been in the centre of the hall with the spectators all round. On these occasions "houses" made of wood and canvas (rather resembling our Punch and Judy booths) might stand on the stage, each representing a different location, such as a palace, a shop, a private house, and it would be clear from the position of the actors in relation to the houses where the scene was taking place.

The Companies.—All the public theatres were built outside the City of London, at Shoreditch or Bankside, because of the hostility of the City authorities who thought that play acting was immoral, that the theatres provided a meeting place for undesirables, and also that they contributed to the spread of the plague. Partly to protect themselves from this hostility, the companies of players put themselves under the protection of a powerful lord whose name they took and whose livery they were entitled to wear. The Lord Chamberlain's Men, the Admiral's Men, and Worcester's Men were the three most important companies.

The regular members of these companies had shares in them, and would receive profits according to their share capital; other actors might be hired for a period. The boys who played the women's parts (there were no actresses on the stage at that time) were apprenticed to one or other of the "sharers". The companies often had their own dramatists from whom they bought plays outright (to-day a company pays a hire-fee or royalty) and it might be that the dramatist was both an actor and sharer as was Shakespeare with the Chamberlain's (later called the King's) Men. It was not the usual practice to print plays: for one thing they were not regarded as literature; for another, printing made them easily available to other theatres. As it was, an actor leaving one company might remember, if imperfectly, the words of a play in which he had taken part, so that the rival company he joined could perform a version of it. Under certain circumstances, however, plays, including these mangled versions, were printed. Companies hard hit by the plague might want ready money (this happened in 1694); or they might decide to get what money they could from the publication of a play of theirs already being performed or even sold by their rivals.

At the end of the sixteenth century the boys' companies such as those of St Paul's (choir) School, and of the Chapel Royal, with their performances in the private theatres, challenged the popularity of the adult companies. The Chapel Children at the Blackfriars, giving plays specially written for them by the great Ben Jonson, were a particularly serious threat which only came to an end in 1608 when the King's Men successfully negotiated to take over the theatre.

HAMLET

When Shakespeare wrote *Hamlet*, it is probable that his main intentions included none of the subtle reasons which his modern critics have discovered. After all, he wrote plays to make a living, and plays of a similar kind had proved very popular. We often forget this when discussing Shakespeare's plays—that he usually chose a story or *plot* which he could be sure would appeal to his audience, by providing action or conflict; not necessarily violent physical action, but, for example, the clash and contrast of personality to be heard in good dialogue.

If this were all that Shakespeare had to offer us, however, his plays would not have retained their fame and popularity for so long. As literary criticism developed, so the critics became more and more aware of the gallery of vividly portrayed *characters* in Shakespeare's plays. At least while the play is being performed, we are ready to believe in the men and women whom Shakespeare presents to us, and some people have felt them to be so "real" that they speak of them almost as if they were human beings instead of the creations of a dramatist's imagination. This has been especially true of Hamlet, whom critics found such a fascinating object of study that conjectures as to his life before the play opens have been conducted as if he had really lived. We shall have to deal with this subject, and the central question of the reason for Hamlet's delay in revenging his father's murder, but we must be careful not to be led into thinking that Hamlet's character *is* the play. There are other elements to consider.

When a modern play is performed, the dramatist can expect the producer to use the resources of the modern theatre to create the right atmosphere. Scenery and lighting can both supplement the text of the play. Shakespeare, however, had to rely upon words alone, and this is one reason why his plays are so rich in *imagery*. The poetic speech is not merely decorative; it reveals character and motive, and indicates how we are to react to a situation or event. For example, Ophelia's death by drowning could hardly be shown on the stage, and, if it were, would be horrible to watch; when we hear of it from Gertrude, we feel sorrow, but our final impression is of beauty and sweetness. Even when he wishes to tell us the time, Shakespeare can evoke in us a visual image—

> But look, the morn, in russet mantle clad,
> Walks o'er the dew of yon high eastward hill.   (I. i. 166-7)

We see, then, that a good dramatist shows us credible people involved in some sort of action; that is, he portrays life. No matter how much he tries, he cannot avoid presenting it in a way that *he* sees it; though determined to be impartial, he cannot avoid selecting certain things to show us, and omitting others. This means that he is expressing his own view of life, his "values", and a great dramatist will have some worthwhile *theme* to offer in this way. *Hamlet* is a particular, individual expression of certain general ideas and intuitions about life which Shakespeare was, perhaps only vaguely, aware of, and it was the need to express these thoughts and emotions which drove him to write the play in the way he did. He had to please an audience, but while doing so he used his dramatic art to convey his own insights into life.

The Plot.—The story of Hamlet is an old one, going back at least to a thirteenth century version, but it is probable that Shakespeare derived his plot from a play which has been lost, but which was known well enough to be alluded to once or twice in contemporary writings. It was clearly a blood-thirsty tragedy on the Senecan model, and was quite probably written by Thomas Kyd, the author of the *Spanish Tragedy*, a play with similar melodramatic features.

Shakespeare's *Hamlet* partakes of these features, though we are prone to forget them as we remember the intellectual, sensitive side to the Prince's character. There is a ghost who returns from the grave with a harrowing account of purgatory, and of a terrible murder to be avenged; the hero feigns madness; the villain is revealed through a contrived play; a girl goes mad and is drowned; her father is stabbed to death while eavesdropping; there is a quarrel in an open grave; the stage is at last littered with corpses who have been poisoned or stabbed. These are the elements which the earlier play provided, and which no doubt account for its immediate popularity. It is a pity that we have no idea of the form of the original play, for it might have given help with the interpretation of Shakespeare's version, by revealing his intentions through the changes he made. As it is, some critics think that the play is a failure because Shakespeare was unable to impose his own scheme upon the material of the primitive revenge play.

Whether we accept this or not, there is still a great deal to admire in Shakespeare's handling of the plot. There is no finer opening scene in all English drama than that on the guard-platform of Elsinore Castle, and it is made even more effective by the contrast with the two scenes which follow. With its variety of pace, through the sharpening and slackening of dramatic tension, the play keeps an audience continually alert, as they follow the hero's moods, which range from intense excitement to utter despondency. This, alone, would have been an achievement, to create such a compelling atmosphere for each episode in the plot, but in addition Shakespeare convinces us that the characters involved in this melodramatic structure are credible.

Apart from considering the source for the plot of the play, critics have tried to find sources for Hamlet's philosophy, and it is generally believed that Shakespeare owed something to Florio's translation of Montaigne's Essays, the first edition of which was published in 1603. To justify this theory, however, we have to assume that Shakespeare saw the translation in MS. before it was published. This is not impossible, but on the other hand, there does not seem to be any good reason why we should not give Shakespeare the credit for having formed the ideas himself.

It is interesting to notice how Shakespeare treats the background to the play. He takes pains to set the scene in Denmark, by continually referring to the country and its inhabitants by name, and showing considerable knowledge of contemporary Danish life. He refers to their intemperance; their national instrument, the kettledrum; their favourite university, Wittenburg. The Castle of Elsinore itself had only recently been built. Yet the play contains several references to events of interest to the Elizabethans, notably the defence of Ostend in 1601 by Sir Francis Vere, and the rivalry between the boys' companies and the adults in the theatre.

So Shakespeare, though lending interest to the play by giving it a setting abroad, does not adhere slavishly to this purpose. If the audience can be moved by or interested in *Hamlet* by an awareness of contemporary events which are relevant, then Shakespeare writes them into the pattern of his play.

The Characters.—From the first, study of the play has tended to concentrate on the character of Hamlet himself, the problem being the reason for his delaying his vengeance so long. Hamlet wonders at his own weakness, and many critics find his excuse for sparing Claudius in the "prayer scene" (III. iii) unconvincing. Also, we are clearly meant to see a comparison between the prince on the one hand, and Fortinbras and Laertes on the other. Fortinbras is the man of action, ready "to find quarrel in a straw" (IV. iv. 55), while Laertes is ready and able to raise the people against Claudius when his father is murdered (IV. v). Hamlet, for a reason unknown even to himself, is unable to act likewise.

Some critics, referring back to the stage conventions of the period, regard the play as still being a revenge melodrama, and assert that there is no real delay because Hamlet could not overcome the external difficulties in his way. There is no mention of such difficulties in the play, however, while Hamlet himself says that he has "the strength and means" to revenge himself (IV. iv. 45) in the scene before Laertes shows how it *could* be done. Nor can we accept Hamlet's doubts about the ghost as the full explanation, for it is not until two months have passed that it suddenly occurs to him to doubt it (II. ii. 582). Altogether, this explanation fails to take into account the complexity of Hamlet's character, and leaves us wondering what there can be in the play to have fascinated audiences and critics for so long.

One interesting approach regards Shakespeare's plays as essentially of their age. Shakespeare's audience did not expect convincing characters, but excitement, so that the plays are written as pieces of stage craft, in which, through sheer dramatic skill, we are made to accept characters or situations which are outrageously but excitingly unreal. Thus, without explanation, we accept Hamlet's delay as if it were real, though the reason for it is purely dramatic—to keep the play going for the necessary five acts! The excitement of the play, according to this theory, is the startling contrast between what Hamlet *is*, a noble, sensitive prince, and what he *does*, goes mad and commits murder. In view of the confusion among the critics over this play, such a theory has its attractions, but it does debase Shakespeare's art to something like a conjuring trick which could hardly have stood the test of time.

The explanations most widely accepted usually rest upon some sort of character trait in the prince. Of these, the first was the opinion that Shakespeare was depicting "a great deed laid upon a soul unequal to the performance of it". Goethe, who suggested this interpretation, saw Hamlet as "a beautiful, pure, noble, and most moral nature, without the strength of nerve which makes the hero". The objection to such a view is that it fails to take into account many of Hamlet's actions which demonstrate his courage, and reduces him to a mere sentimental weakling.

Fairly close to this one, is a theory made popular by Coleridge, who said, "We see a great, an almost enormous, intellectual activity and a proportionate aversion to real action consequent upon it, with all its symptoms and accompanying qualities. This character Shakespeare places in circumstances under which it is obliged to act on the spur of the moment: Hamlet is brave and careless of death, but he vacillates from sensibility and procrastinates from thought, and loses the power of action in the energy of resolve." This is really one explanation which Hamlet himself thinks of, when he fears that it may be

> "some craven scruple
> Of thinking too precisely on th' event."   (IV. iv. 40-1)

It is unsatisfactory because it ignores the fact that there is something wrong with Hamlet *before* he is given the task by the Ghost; it takes no account of his first soliloquy (I. ii. 129-59).

The same objection can be made to the idea that Hamlet is a man of modern moral sensibility, unable because of his noble nature to commit murder, even in revenge. We may add, too, that Hamlet never for a moment doubts the righteousness of his vengeance.

Indeed, if we are to look at Hamlet's mind at all, it is essential to begin with his first soliloquy, which shows that he is in an abnormal state of mind, that he is undergoing a period of great mental strain. For a close analysis, along these lines, of Hamlet's character and state of mind, reference should be made to A. C. Bradley, *Shakespearean Tragedy*, an indispensable book for any serious student of *Hamlet*. If Bradley errs, it is in too close a study of events and situations *outside* the play, and in a rather too literal approach to what is, after all a *poetic* drama. Briefly, he sees Hamlet as intellectual, contemplative, highly emotional, and endowed with keen moral sensibility. When Hamlet's father dies, he is passed over in favour of Claudius in the election to the vacant throne, but, worse than all this, his mother marries this uncle whom Hamlet despises, and so commits incest. Under the blow of this tremendous moral shock, he sinks into a state which he himself describes as "weakness and melancholy" (II. ii. 585). The news, from his father's ghost, that Claudius is a murderer is almost too much, and Hamlet's reason almost gives way; he is hysterical in his passion. This feeling is what suggests to him the plan of feigning madness in order to go to work, but after this, his energy sapped by the melancholia induced by his situation, he sinks into dejection and apathy, to be roused only when he is forced by circumstance to act.

Much of this account is admirable, and if any fault is apparent, it no doubt lies in the summary, and not in Bradley's work. Nevertheless, there are two points that need to be made. One is that it relies upon rather elementary ideas of psychology, involving the vague diagnosis of "melancholia". Secondly, the argument relies upon Hamlet's having a refined moral sensibility, the only evidence of which is that the argument states it is shocked by the events of the first act. The argument at this point is a circular one: Hamlet has a refined moral sensibility because he is shocked, and he is shocked because he has a refined moral sensibility. On the other hand, there is evidence (in his gibes and sneers at Polonius, his indifference to the latter's death, his still greater callousness towards the deaths of Rosencrantz and Guildenstern, his crude invective of Ophelia, and his violence and threats to his mother) that his moral sensibility is no more refined than that of most other characters in the play.

This seeming impasse has led T. S. Eliot to write that Hamlet is "dominated by an emotion . . . in excess of the facts as they appear". It almost suggests that we are wrong to look for a motive of this sort in Hamlet, and some critics assert that this is the case. If we persist, however, there is one direction in which the problem can be pursued. Modern psychiatry is the study of complex states of mind in which the motives of action are suppressed and therefore hidden from the conscious mind, and an analysis of Hamlet's situation and conduct from this point of view is at the least interesting.

His first soliloquy is marked by horror at his mother's re-marriage, and it is suggested that this is because it arouses in him memories of his early childhood, when he first repressed, because of filial piety and other social influences, his jealousy of his own father, a jealousy which was so strong that he perhaps even desired to kill his father. Such "complexes", as they are called, have been observed, and a mother's re-marriage has been known to cause deep mental disturbance, "in excess of the facts". Of course, it is not suggested that Shakespeare understood this himself, but he observed and depicted life, and there is no reason why he should not have observed this condition and then portrayed it. If there *is* a psychological explanation, it would seem to lie somewhere here.

No doubt the debate will continue undecided, as long as *Hamlet* is studied. There is no *right* way of approaching a play by Shakespeare, and each of the views discussed contains elements which are useful for an understanding of the play. The bibliography in Appendix II lists the more important analyses of Hamlet's character.

We can regard the other characters as standing in opposition and contrast to the play's central figure. "Something is rotten in the state of Denmark" (I. iv. 90) and each of the characters in some measure partakes of the evil. This accounts in some measure for Hamlet's revulsion and bitterness.

Horatio is the exception, who stands for those values which Hamlet most admires—probably because he himself lacks them—and Hamlet's praise (III. ii. 60-9) sums him up almost completely. Apart from this, Horatio serves as a confidant, a character to whom the hero can talk freely, and so reveal himself to the audience. For this reason, there are inconsistencies in him, for example, in his knowledge of Denmark. He can tell Danish troops why Denmark is preparing for war (I. i) and yet has to be told about Danish drinking habits (I. iv. 7-22).

Claudius is the centre of the corruption which pollutes Denmark, yet he is not such a tremendously evil man as Hamlet would have us believe. He is rather a cunning schemer than a deep and subtle villain, never looking very far forward in his plans. We can despise him chiefly for his intemperance, his lack of real feeling, his utter selfishness. He has real ability, nevertheless, as we see in the Council scene (I. ii) when he deals with state affairs, and he is prompt and resourceful in producing a new plan to deal with Hamlet when he finds that the journey to England has failed (IV. vii). Moreover, he shows real dignity and courage when Laertes breaks upon him in revolt (IV. v). It is his hypocrisy, however, which is his greatest evil power. He can use all his talents to create an easy confident manner, and hide his sins under a smiling, ingratiating appearance.

Whether knowingly or not, *Polonius* supports this usurper, and we can see that it is not inappropriate, for he, too, is a kind of hypocrite. His advice to Laertes (I. iii. 55-81) shows a worldly morality which is based largely upon appearances, and at the opening of II. i, he shows the same concern for reputation, without bothering at all about the reality. He prefers to secure his ends by crooked means, and his mania for eavesdropping proves his undoing. Unable to believe any better of others than of himself, he sets his estimate of human nature very low. Dramatically, he very often serves, by his comic garrulity, to relieve the tragic tension, and to provide a target for some of Hamlet's more pointed satirical remarks when he is feigning madness.

Laertes is a true son of this worldly, easy-going father, delivering a priggish lecture to his sister which reveals an equally suspicious nature (I. iii. 5-44). With all the outward accomplishments of his age, he is nevertheless quite without principle, so that although he suffers losses as great as Hamlet, he never wins our sympathy. He is clearly intended to be a complete contrast to Hamlet. He is above all things a man of action, with a mind untroubled by scruples or doubts of any kind. In the same position as Hamlet he at once seeks for vengeance, completely indifferent as to how it is to be secured. Such a nature would have felt little shock at a mother's infidelity—provided it was not made public.

These three, Claudius, Polonius, and Laertes, together with Rosencrantz and Guildenstern and Osric, show how the outward forms of behaviour can hide inner realities of character, while Hamlet on the other hand, will have nothing to do with such hypocrisy: "Seems, madam! Nay it is; I know not seems" (I. ii. 76). The women, too, though never faced with real moral choices, have the same easy attitude to general behaviour.

Gertrude is without any depth of character, accepting life uncritically as it comes. Her chief trait is a readiness to give affection, for she loves her son and Claudius, and no doubt gave the same love to her former husband. Though sensual and weak in character, she is probably no criminal. Hamlet deliberately charges her with her husband's death (III. iv. 31), but the fact that she does not appear to understand him suggests that she is innocent.

Ophelia is unfortunate in that she lacks guidance, for as we have seen, Polonius is too lax with his children, and then, with his base suspicions, forces her to avoid Hamlet altogether. She is quite lost in this world of intrigue and deceit, and her innocence is even used by her own father in his stratagems (III. i). Young, beautiful, and amiable, she is also virtuous, but having no will of her own, no strength of mind, she is led into the plot against Hamlet. She could hardly have acted otherwise, believing as she did that Hamlet was mad and that she was really trying to help him. The sadness and pathos of her fate win our sympathy completely, so that in the end we forgive any faults she may have. Her death is without purpose or justification, demonstrating the blind destructiveness of the evil in Denmark.

Hamlet's treatment of her raises problems over which there will probably never be complete agreement. It is fairly certain that he did have a serious affection for her, but his own troubles, and her sudden breaking off of their relationship are enough to alter his attitude. His visit to her room (II. i. 75-100) was perhaps to take farewell of her, more possibly to seek help and comfort which she was incapable of giving. In any case, Hamlet felt that from then on he was alone, and that Ophelia, too, was unreliable like his mother: "Frailty, thy name is woman!" (I. ii. 146). After this, he expresses his disgust for the sex in terms which demonstrate a strong sexual bias such as tends to confirm the theory of his conduct suggested by modern psycho-analysis.

The Language and Imagery.—As we have seen, Hamlet is concerned in a fight against an evil which is concealed from view, while he is himself assailed by some unknown, incomprehensible mental disorder. The imagery of the play indicates this through images of disease, especially of hidden complaints. Thus Hamlet warns his mother to avoid believing that his madness makes him accuse her:

> It will but skin and film the ulcerous place,
> Whiles rank corruption mining all within,
> Infects unseen.   (III. iv. 149-51)

Claudius, does not say "to the point", but "to the quick of

th' ulcer" (IV. vii. 124) in a speech which refers also to pleurisy and to the belief that sighs are physically harmful because they use up blood. Elsewhere, he says of Hamlet: "like the hectic (*i.e.* fever) in my blood he rages" (IV. iii. 65), while Hamlet spares him with the words: "This physic but prolongs thy sickly days" (III. iii. 96). A speech which has often been taken to apply to Hamlet's own condition contains similar reference to physical defects: "some vicious mole of nature" and "the o'ergrowth of some complexion" (I. iv. 23-38).

In fact, all kinds of corruption abound, and they are given a central "reference point" in the scene when Hamlet discusses death and the corruption of the body with the gravedigger in V. i, and when the fate of a corrupt soul is described by the Ghost (I. v. 9-20).

In his first soliloquy, Hamlet calls the world "An unweeded garden, That grows to seed" (I. ii. 135-6) and warns his mother not to "spread the compost on the weeds, To make them ranker" (III. iv. 153-4). This image of the world as a garden is more important, however, for the positive values of beauty and virtue it provides, through the references to flowers. Gertrude's marriage to Claudius "takes off the rose From the fair forehead of an innocent love" (III. iv. 44-5). More obviously, Ophelia is associated with these images. Hamlet's love for her, says her brother, is "a violet in the youth of primy nature" (I. iii. 7) and he goes on:

> The canker galls the infants of the spring
> Too oft before their buttons be disclos'd;
> And in the morn and liquid dew of youth
> Contagious blastments are most imminent.   (39-42)

In three more scenes, Ophelia is associated with flowers: when she appears, mad, before her brother (IV. v. 172-85); when Gertrude recounts the manner of her death (IV. vii. 167-84); and at her funeral (V. i. 222-36). Such associations stress her beauty, innocence and helplessness in the corrupt world of Elsinore.

It has already been mentioned that Hamlet harps continually on sexual matters, and much of it is done through puns. Dr

Johnson said of Shakespeare that "a quibble was to him the fatal Cleopatra for which he lost the world and was content to lose it" and a modern audience might agree that Shakespeare's characters make puns in the most unlikely situations. We should remember, however, that people tend to make jokes when under a severe nervous strain, and that puns were not necessarily weak jokes, but demonstrated the ironies of life, and subtle relationships between ideas. Thus Hamlet's first line: "A little more than kin, and less than kind" (I. ii. 65) shows a bitter awareness of the ambiguity in the attitude of Claudius (he appears *kind*, but is *unnatural*) and in his relationship (he is both father and uncle, yet worthy to be neither). M. M. Mahood, in *Shakespeare's Word Play*, has pointed out the complex ambiguity in Hamlet's speech about the "dram of eale" which destroys an otherwise fine man (I. iv. 23-38). Each of the terms used have two significances, one suggesting an inner, mental quality, and the other an outward, physical feature. For example, "nature's livery" can be a *gift* of nature (*i.e.* a character trait) or a mark or *badge* (*i.e.* an outward blemish). In the same way, "fortune's star" can be using star in the sense of *blaze*, the name given to a white mark on a horse's forehead. In this way, the puns suggest the uncertainty there is about the sources of man's faults—are the causes physical or mental? No other play of Shakespeare's contains so many puns, and such subtle ones. It appears to be a figure of speech which appealed to Hamlet. His use of the device shows us his swift, keen, subtle, active, and complex mind, and of course, his feigned madness lent itself to the device, for under the guise of nonsense he could make satirical points. Polonius, too, enjoyed playing with words, for example, at I. iii. 105-9, but in his case, we can safely regard his puns as examples of rather enfeebled wit.

The style is marked particularly by its variety. Some of the verse has the speed and power of the greatest tragedies, while other speeches might have come from much earlier plays. For concise, flexible verse narrative, nothing can better the mature, skilful handling of Hamlet's account of his stratagem against Rosencrantz and Guildenstern (V. ii. 1-55). Very often, it is Claudius who is given the verse tight-packed with images typical of the mature style, for example, in III. iii. 36-71. On the other hand, Polonius's precepts to Laertes (I. iii. 55-81), and Gertrude's description of Ophelia's death (IV. viii. 167-84) are earlier in style in their more conventional rhythms and treatment.

Most notable is the amount of prose in the play. It is usually used in Shakespeare in scenes involving inferiors and comic characters (*e.g.* the Grave-diggers and Osric). It is used also for light and flippant conversation, or to mark a lower dramatic note before or after scenes of higher pitch (*e.g.* III. ii., where it follows the violent scene between Hamlet and Ophelia, and precedes the tense play scene which is to test Claudius's guilt). Finally, Elizabethan stage convention dictated that madmen should speak prose, so that Hamlet feigning madness, and Ophelia when she is really mad both speak prose.

Themes.—So far, we have approached the play through the main character, but this can be a very limiting method of interpretation, and in this century, critics have been concerned with several other aspects. For example, since it is based on a revenge play, possibly *Hamlet* is a development of the type. By his doubts and delays, Hamlet is involved in the process of achieving the proper state of mind for a "just" revenge. At first, he is swept away by passion; finally, he becomes "the scourge and minister" (III. iv. 175) of Heaven. This is a more subtle variation on the idea that Hamlet is too hindered by moral scruple to take vengeance on Claudius.

A very revealing aspect of the play is the way in which the other characters are grouped round the central figure. In particular, it is clear that we are meant to compare Hamlet with Horatio as well as Laertes and Fortinbras. Laertes is the social, gentlemanly ideal, and we have seen how far he falls short of perfection. Fortinbras represents the virtues of the soldier, and he too is not without his faults of pride and hardness. Though Hamlet uses Fortinbras's expedition to spur his dull revenge, he comments unfavourably on the waste of so many fine lives (IV. iv). All things considered, the standards of scholarly good manners and acceptance of the world provided by Horatio are attractive in the context, and possibly they are what Shakespeare meant us to see as the solution to Hamlet's problem. From such a view are derived most of the interpretations which regard the play as an examination of modes of conduct, or of morals. These characters point to the various ways in which Hamlet can choose to act—a choice which he raises in his meditations:

> Whether 'tis nobler in the mind to suffer
> The slings and arrows of outrageous fortune,
> Or to take arms against a sea of troubles,
> And by opposing end them? (III. i. 57-60)

A brief glance at the imagery has shown that character analysis is not the only way to look at the play. In the references to hidden corruption and garden weeds, is a suggestion that we can look at the play as a struggle by an individual against the corruptions and social evils around him, a struggle which we all, in some measure, have to carry on.

Hamlet's pre-occupation with the evil in the world, and his hesitation over revenge, have led many people to see him as the representative of Man, faced with moral choices, evil, and ultimately death. Some have even seen, in his scruples, indications that he can see salvation only in Christianity. It is certainly true that Hamlet ponders each of these three major aspects of life and it is an attractive idea that the play is a more modern version of *Everyman*. If it is true, as Professor C. S. Lewis has said, "that the real and lasting mystery of our human situation has been greatly depicted" in *Hamlet*, then much is explained. Hamlet is each one of us, and so we all see ourselves in Hamlet. This is why there have been so many interpretations, for we are all explaining ourselves. And in support of this there is Hazlitt, who over a hundred years ago wrote, "It is we who are Hamlet", and there is the fact that many men, including Coleridge, described themselves very well when interpreting the character of the prince.

It is the imagery, too, which leads Professor Wilson Knight to his view of Shakespeare's plays as "extended metaphors", and his interpretations are always illuminating. He says of Hamlet that because he is associated with a ghost of evil omen, and is subject to heart-sickness and melancholy, he is the "ambassador of death". The court may be tawdry and superficial in its morals, but it is at least tolerant, and for the most part *normal*, in contrast with Hamlet's over-sensitivity. In fact, Ophelia, as a member of the court, reveals positive virtues through the imagery of purity and sweetness associated with her, and Hamlet destroys her. The central question of the play, then, is the opposition between easy acceptance of life (Claudius, Polonius, Gertrude), and complete rejection and disgust (Hamlet). The solution is suggested in two ways: Horatio's acceptance of life, which is based on understanding, not mere unthinking indulgence; and the play scene, which shows the importance of "control" (emphasised especially by Hamlet's advice to the actors—III. ii. 1-41). Both of these hint at the Christian ethic as the only positive solution, though Professor Knight insists we should not credit Hamlet with a realisation of the fact.

Whatever we believe, we shall never agree, for there is no one correct interpretation of the play. There are elements of truth in every approach to its problems, but Hamlet himself has shown us our error: "Why, look you now, how unworthy a thing you make of me! You would play upon me; you would seem to know my stops; you would pluck out the heart of my mystery. . . . Call me what instrument you will, though you can fret me, yet you cannot play upon me" (III. ii. 346-54).

HAMLET

DRAMATIS PERSONAE

CLAUDIUS, King of Denmark.

HAMLET, son to the former and nephew to the present King.

POLONIUS, Lord Chamberlain.

HORATIO, friend to Hamlet.

LAERTES, son to Polonius.

VOLTEMAND,
CORNELIUS,
ROSENCRANTZ,
GUILDENSTERN,   } courtiers.
OSRIC,
A GENTLEMAN,

A PRIEST.

MARCELLUS, } officers.
BERNARDO,

FRANCISCO, a soldier.

REYNALDO, servant to Polonius.

PLAYERS.

TWO CLOWNS, grave-diggers.

FORTINBRAS, Prince of Norway.

A NORWEGIAN CAPTAIN.

ENGLISH AMBASSADORS.

GERTRUDE, Queen of Denmark, and mother of Hamlet.

OPHELIA, daughter to Polonius.

GHOST OF HAMLET'S FATHER.

LORDS, LADIES, OFFICERS, SOLDIERS, SAILORS, MESSENGERS, and ATTENDANTS.

SCENE: *Denmark.*

ACT I

SCENE I. *Elsinore. The guard-platform of the Castle.*

FRANCISCO *at his post. Enter to him* BERNARDO.

Ber. Who 's there?

Fran. Nay, answer me. Stand and unfold yourself.

Ber. Long live the King!

Fran. Bernardo?

Ber. He.   5

Fran. You come most carefully upon your hour.

Ber. 'Tis now struck twelve; get thee to bed, Francisco.

Fran. For this relief much thanks. 'Tis bitter cold,
And I am sick at heart.

Ber. Have you had quiet guard?

Fran.   Not a mouse stirring.

Ber. Well, good night.   11
If you do meet Horatio and Marcellus,
The rivals of my watch, bid them make haste.

NOTES

ACT I. SCENE I

1. **Who 's there:** The scarcely suppressed, tense expectation of this opening is skilfully conveyed, at once surrounding the action with the atmosphere of mystery and gloom which is characteristic of the play.

2. **answer me:** the emphasis is on *me*. Francisco is on guard, and so entitled to challenge.

3. **Long live the King:** probably the watchword, and dramatically ironic. That Marcellus and Horatio do not use the words (line 15) is probably owing to their agitation.

6. **upon your hour:** just at the appointed time.

8. **much thanks:** many thanks.

13. **rivals:** partners. **bid them make haste:** Bernardo does not want to be left alone.

Enter HORATIO *and* MARCELLUS.

Fran. I think I hear them. Stand ho! Who is there?
Hor. Friends to this ground.
Mar.   And liegemen to the Dane.
Fran. Give you good night.
Mar.   O, farewell, honest soldier!
Who hath reliev'd you?
 Fran.   Bernardo hath my place.   17
Give you good night.   [*Exit.*
 Mar.   Holla, Bernardo!
 Ber.   Say—
What, is Horatio there?
 Hor.   A piece of him.
 Ber. Welcome, Horatio; welcome, good Marcellus. 20
 Hor. What, has this thing appear'd again to-night?
 Ber. I have seen nothing.
 Mar. Horatio says 'tis but our fantasy,
And will not let belief take hold of him
Touching this dreaded sight, twice seen of us;   25
Therefore I have entreated him along
With us to watch the minutes of this night,
That, if again this apparition come,
He may approve our eyes and speak to it.
 Hor. Tush, tush, 'twill not appear.
 Ber.   Sit down awhile, 30
And let us once again assail your ears,
That are so fortified against our story,
What we have two nights seen.
 Hor.   Well, sit we down,
And let us hear Bernardo speak of this.
 Ber. Last night of all,   35
When yond same star that 's westward from the pole
Had made his course t' illume that part of heaven
Where now it burns, Marcellus and myself,
The bell then beating one—

Enter GHOST.

 Mar. Peace, break thee off; look where it comes again. 40

15. **the Dane:** the King of Denmark.
16. **Give you:** may God give you.

19. **A piece of him:** a jesting answer, perhaps intended to show that Horatio, the scholar, is sceptical.
21. **has this thing:** the words are clearly contemptuous, and so spoken by Horatio. Some editors, however, following the First Folio, give the line to Marcellus.
23. **fantasy:** imagination.

29. **approve our eyes:** corroborate the evidence of our eyes. **speak to it:** we are told why Horatio has been asked to do so in line 42.

31. **assail your ears:** try to convince you by telling you (what we have seen on two nights).

33. **sit we down:** let us sit down.

36. **westward from the pole:** west of the Pole star.
37. **his:** its. It is probable that Shakespeare never used *its*, which was just beginning to be used in his day. We find that he sometimes used *it*, *e.g.* in I. ii. 216. **illume:** illuminate.

Ber. In the same figure, like the King that 's dead.

Mar. Thou art a scholar; speak to it, Horatio.

Ber. Looks 'a not like the King? Mark it, Horatio.

Hor. Most like. It harrows me with fear and wonder.

Ber. It would be spoke to.

Mar.   Question it, Horatio.   45

Hor. What art thou that usurp'st this time of night
Together with that fair and warlike form
In which the majesty of buried Denmark
Did sometimes march? By heaven I charge thee, speak!

Mar. It is offended.

Ber.   See, it stalks away.   50

Hor. Stay! speak, speak! I charge thee, speak!

                              [*Exit* GHOST.

Mar. 'Tis gone, and will not answer.

Ber. How now, Horatio! You tremble and look pale.
Is not this something more than fantasy?
What think you on 't?   55

Hor. Before my God, I might not this believe
Without the sensible and true avouch
Of mine own eyes.

Mar.   Is it not like the King?

Hor. As thou art to thyself:
Such was the very armour he had on   60
When he the ambitious Norway combated;
So frown'd he once when, in an angry parle,
He smote the sledded Polacks on the ice.
'Tis strange.

Mar. Thus twice before, and jump at this dead hour,   65
With martial stalk hath he gone by our watch.

Hor. In what particular thought to work I know not;
But, in the gross and scope of mine opinion,
This bodes some strange eruption to our state.

Mar. Good now, sit down, and tell me, he that knows,   70
Why this same strict and most observant watch
So nightly toils the subject of the land;
And why such daily cast of brazen cannon,
And foreign mart for implements of war;

42. **Thou art a scholar:** Latin was the language used in exorcisms and conjurations, so scholars were best fitted to address ghosts. The soldiers presumably did not dare.

43. **'a:** a dialectal form of *he*, indicating colloquial speech.

44. **harrows me:** tortures me, as if being torn by the teeth of a harrow. Notice that Horatio, so far sceptical, has been lost for words.

45. **It would be spoke to:** it wishes to be spoken to. It was believed that ghosts would not speak until first addressed.

46. **usurp'st:** J. Dover Wilson suggests that this is the cause of offence (line 50), by suggesting that the spirit has no *right* to the form of King Hamlet, but the word may merely imply that it is not *natural* for a spirit to appear on earth.

48. **Denmark:** *i.e.* the King of Denmark. Similarly in line 61, *Norway* is used for the King of Norway.

49. **sometimes:** formerly.

56. **might:** could.

57. **sensible and true avouch:** visible and undoubted assurance; *sensible* here means "appealing to the senses".

62. **parle:** parley, or conference. Here, the conference probably became a fight.

63. **sledded Polacks:** the Poles in sleds, or sledges.

65. **jump:** just; exactly.

67. **In what particular thought,** etc.: I cannot form any precise opinion, but my own general view is, etc.

69. **eruption:** outbreak of violence. The word, however, suggests also the breaking out of disease or of a boil, adding to the disease imagery which pervades the play.

70. **Good now:** now, my good friends.

72. **toils the subject:** makes the people toil.

74. **mart:** purchase; marketing.

Why such impress of shipwrights, whose sore task   75
Does not divide the Sunday from the week;
What might be toward, that this sweaty haste
Doth make the night joint-labourer with the day.
Who is 't that can inform me?
   Hor.   That can I;
At least, the whisper goes so. Our last king,   80
Whose image even but now appear'd to us,
Was, as you know, by Fortinbras of Norway,
Thereto prick'd on by a most emulate pride,
Dar'd to the combat; in which our valiant Hamlet—
For so this side of our known world esteem'd him—   85
Did slay this Fortinbras; who, by a seal'd compact,
Well ratified by law and heraldry,
Did forfeit, with his life, all those his lands
Which he stood seiz'd of, to the conqueror;
Against the which a moiety competent   90
Was gaged by our king! which had return'd
To the inheritance of Fortinbras,
Had he been vanquisher; as, by the same comart
And carriage of the article design'd,
His fell to Hamlet. Now, sir, young Fortinbras,   95
Of unimproved mettle hot and full,
Hath in the skirts of Norway, here and there,
Shark'd up a list of lawless resolutes,
For food and diet, to some enterprise
That hath a stomach in 't; which is no other,   100
As it doth well appear unto our state,
But to recover of us, by strong hand
And terms compulsatory, those foresaid lands
So by his father lost; and this, I take it,
Is the main motive of our preparations,   105
The source of this our watch, and the chief head
Of this post-haste and romage in the land.
   Ber. I think it be no other but e'en so.
Well may it sort, that this portentous figure
Comes armed through our watch; so like the King   110
That was and is the question of these wars.

75. **impress**: enlistment; forced service. **whose sore task . . . week**: whose work is so urgent that they are forced to work on Sunday as if it were any other day of the week. Marcellus goes on to say that they work all night, too.

77. **toward**: impending.

83. **prick'd on by . . . pride**: spurred on by a very emulous pride.

84. **valiant Hamlet**: *i.e.* the late King, not the hero of the play.

87. **Well ratified . . . heraldry**: made binding by both the laws of nations and the laws of honour and chivalry. It is possible, however, that *law and heraldry* is hendiadys equivalent to *the law of heraldry*.

90. **a moiety competent**: a portion of equal value.

91-2. **which had return'd . . . Fortinbras**: which would have become the possession of Fortinbras. We find this old use of *inheritance* surviving in the *Book of Common Prayer*, in "Bless thine inheritance".

93-4. **by the same comart . . . design'd**: by the same joint bargain and the clause drawn up on the point.

96. **unimproved**: untutored, or perhaps, unemployed, not turned to good account.

97. **skirts**: outskirts, where men would be more lawless, owing to their distance from the centre of government.

98. **Shark'd up**: picked up indiscriminately as a shark picks up food. The image is meant to convey the bloodthirsty nature of the resolutes or desperadoes whom Fortinbras has assembled, and who require no pay but their keep, *food and diet*.

99-100. **some enterprise . . . in 't**: some undertaking requiring courage to carry out. *Stomach* in the sense of "courage" is common in Shakespeare, but the words *food and diet* suggest a play on the other meaning.

101. **state**: government.

103. **compulsatory**: imposed by force.

106. **head**: cause; source. The metaphor is from the head or source of a river.

107. **romage**: bustle.

109. **Well may it sort**: it is most fitting. Bernardo feels that the ghost is an omen of trouble, while Horatio in line 112 belittles it, though confirming that such things are possible by quoting more spectacular examples.

Hor.   A mote it is to trouble the mind's eye.
In the most high and palmy state of Rome,
A little ere the mightiest Julius fell,
The graves stood tenantless, and the sheeted dead   115
Did squeak and gibber in the Roman streets;
As, stars with trains of fire, and dews of blood,
Disasters in the sun; and the moist star
Upon whose influence Neptune's empire stands
Was sick almost to doomsday with eclipse;   120
And even the like precurse of fear'd events,
As harbingers preceding still the fates
And prologue to the omen coming on,
Have heaven and earth together demonstrated
Unto our climatures and countrymen.   125

Re-enter GHOST.

But, soft, behold! Lo, where it comes again!
I 'll cross it, though it blast me.   Stay, illusion.
                              [GHOST *spreads its arms.*
If thou hast any sound or use of voice,
Speak to me.
If there be any good thing to be done,   130
That may to thee do ease and grace to me,
Speak to me.
If thou art privy to thy country's fate,
Which happily foreknowing may avoid,
O, speak!   135
Or if thou hast uphoarded in thy life
Extorted treasure in the womb of earth,
For which, they say, you spirits oft walk in death,
                              [*The cock crows.*
Speak of it.   Stay, and speak.   Stop it, Marcellus.
     Mar.   Shall I strike at it with my partisan?   140
     Hor.   Do, if it will not stand.
     Ber.   'Tis here!
     Hor.   'Tis here!
     Mar.   'Tis gone!   [*Exit* GHOST.
We do it wrong, being so majestical,

113. **palmy state**: flourishing commonwealth. In many of his tragedies, Shakespeare plays upon the superstitious belief in astrology and omens held by his audience. The night before the assassination of Caesar in *Julius Caesar* is stormy, and wonders are said to take place, just as after King Duncan's death in *Macbeth*, we hear of unnatural events and a terrible storm. Even if we cannot believe in such things, their effect in the play is to widen and deepen the significance of the action. For the omens that follow, Shakespeare is indebted to North's translation of Plutarch's *Lives* and Marlowe's translation of Lucan's *Pharsalia*, Book I. Those of lines 117-20, however, appear to be contemporary references, for there were two total lunar eclipses visible in England in 1598, and solar eclipses in 1598, 1600, and 1601.

114. **mightiest**: most mighty.

117. **As stars**, etc.: A line has probably been dropped out between this line and the previous one. J. Dover Wilson, however, suggests transposing lines 117-20 to follow 125.

118. **Disasters**: unfavourable aspects. The word was originally an astrological term denoting an aspect of a star or planet whose influence brought misfortune. **moist star**: the moon, which was supposed to suck up moisture from the earth, and which causes the tides.

119. **Upon whose ... stands**: upon whose power depends the sovereignty of Neptune (who is god of the oceans). **influence** is another astrological term, denoting the supposed power of the celestial bodies over events on earth, men's lives and characters.

120. **sick almost to doomsday**: It was as dark as if the Day of Judgment were at hand.

121. **precurse**: heralding.

122. **still**: always.

123. **omen**: *i.e.* calamity; event (foretold by the omen).

125. **climatures**: regions.

127. **though it blast me**: Horatio alludes to the superstition that anyone who crossed the path of a ghost fell under a malignant influence.

134. **happily**: perchance.

140. **partisan**: a kind of halberd, about five or six feet long, for both striking and thrusting. The head consisted of a battle-axe blade, balanced by a hook, and the whole terminated in a spike like a spear.

To offer it the show of violence;
For it is, as the air, invulnerable,   145
And our vain blows malicious mockery.
   Ber. It was about to speak, when the cock crew.
   Hor. And then it started like a guilty thing
Upon a fearful summons. I have heard
The cock, that is the trumpet to the morn,   150
Doth with his lofty and shrill-sounding throat
Awake the god of day; and at his warning,
Whether in sea or fire, in earth or air,
Th' extravagant and erring spirit hies
To his confine; and of the truth herein   155
This present object made probation.
   Mar. It faded on the crowing of the cock.
Some say that ever 'gainst that season comes
Wherein our Saviour's birth is celebrated,
This bird of dawning singeth all night long;   160
And then, they say, no spirit dare stir abroad,
The nights are wholesome, then no planets strike,
No fairy takes, nor witch hath power to charm,
So hallowed and so gracious is that time.
   Hor. So have I heard, and do in part believe it.   165
But look, the morn, in russet mantle clad,
Walks o'er the dew of yon high eastward hill.
Break we our watch up; and, by my advice,
Let us impart what we have seen to-night
Unto young Hamlet; for, upon my life,   170
This spirit, dumb to us, will speak to him.
Do you consent we shall acquaint him with it,
As needful in our loves, fitting our duty?
   Mar. Let 's do 't, I pray; and I this morning know
Where we shall find him most convenient.   [*Exeunt.*

153-5. **Whether in sea . . . confine:** There were thought to be four elements: air, earth, fire, and water, in which belonged various spirits. If such spirits were **extravagant,** i.e. *wandering beyond bounds* or **erring,** i.e. *straying*, they had to return at cock-crow to their **confine,** or *proper limits.*

156. **made probation:** afforded proof.

158. **ever 'gainst:** always when.

162. **no planets strike:** no planets exert an evil influence. This is yet another technical term from astrology.

163. **takes:** bewitches.

164. **gracious:** blessed; benign.

165. **in part believe:** Horatio again shows himself the sceptic.

166. **russet:** a coarse, homespun cloth of grey or reddish colour.

Scene II.   *Elsinore.   The Castle.*

Flourish.   Enter Claudius King of Denmark, Gertrude
the Queen, *and* Councillors, *including* Polonius, *his son*
Laertes, Voltemand, Cornelius, *and* Hamlet.

King. Though yet of Hamlet our dear brother's death
The memory be green; and that it us befitted
To bear our hearts in grief, and our whole kingdom
To be contracted in one brow of woe;
Yet so far hath discretion fought with nature   5
That we with wisest sorrow think on him,
Together with remembrance of ourselves.
Therefore our sometime sister, now our queen,
Th' imperial jointress to this warlike state,
Have we, as 'twere with a defeated joy,   10
With an auspicious and a dropping eye,
With mirth in funeral, and with dirge in marriage,
In equal scale weighing delight and dole,
Taken to wife; nor have we herein barr'd
Your better wisdoms, which have freely gone   15
With this affair along.   For all, our thanks.
Now follows that you know: young Fortinbras,
Holding a weak supposal of our worth,
Or thinking by our late dear brother's death
Our state to be disjoint and out of frame,   20
Co-leagued with this dream of his advantage—
He hath not fail'd to pester us with message
Importing the surrender of those lands
Lost by his father, with all bands of law,
To our most valiant brother.   So much for him.   25
Now for ourself, and for this time of meeting,
Thus much the business is: we have here writ
To Norway, uncle of young Fortinbras—
Who, impotent and bed-rid, scarcely hears
Of this his nephew's purpose—to suppress   30
His further gait herein, in that the levies,
The lists, and full proportions, are all made
Out of his subject; and we here dispatch

ACT I. SCENE II

Stage direction: Notice that Hamlet enters last in his suit of "solemn black", standing out starkly against the pomp and glitter of this pleasure-loving court, which itself, of course, provides a strong contrast to the previous scene.

1. **Though yet:** This speech reveals Claudius as superficially attractive, a fluent orator, holding forth in truly royal fashion on matters of state. When dealing, however, with his brother's death and his own marriage he betrays a certain uneasiness in "the set and pedantically antithetic form of the sentences". His tongue is a little *too* glib, his manner too unctuous to be genuine, though this is a subtlety which an audience would be unaware of when seeing the play for the first time.

2. **that:** used instead of repeating *though*.

3-4. **our whole . . . woe:** it befitted everyone in the kingdom to contract his brow in sorrow.

6-7. **we with wisest . . . ourselves:** Claudius controls his sorrow wisely, thinking of himself as well as of the dead.

8. **sometime:** former.

9. **jointress:** a widow who holds a jointure or life-interest. Thus the position seems to be that Gertrude has inherited the throne on the death of King Hamlet, and Claudius is ruling because he has married her. Some editors, however, take the word to mean merely *partner*.

10. **defeated:** marred; disfigured.

11. **dropping:** weeping.

13. **dole:** sorrow.

14-15. **barr'd . . . along:** excluded your wise counsel which has been freely given in approval of the marriage.

17. **Now follows that:** The speech now takes on a more direct and vigorous style, when plain matters of state are to be dealt with.

18. **supposal:** estimate; opinion.

20. **disjoint and out of frame:** disrupted and out of joint.

21. **Co-leagued . . . advantage:** together with this illusion of superiority (*i.e.* his "supposal of our worth").

23. **Importing:** relating to; concerning.

24. **with all bands of law:** with all legal formalities.

31. **gait:** progress; proceeding. **in that:** inasmuch as.

32. **proportions:** quotas; contingents. Claudius is complaining to the King of Norway because the whole of Fortinbras's army is drawn from Norwegian subjects.

You, good Cornelius, and you, Voltemand,
For bearers of this greeting to old Norway;   35
Giving to you no further personal power
To business with the King more than the scope
Of these delated articles allow.
Farewell; and let your haste commend your duty.

    Cor.
    Vol.   In that and all things will we show our duty.   40

    King.   We doubt it nothing, heartily farewell.
                   [*Exeunt* VOLTEMAND *and* CORNELIUS.

And now, Laertes, what 's the news with you?
You told us of some suit; what is 't, Laertes?
You cannot speak of reason to the Dane
And lose your voice.   What wouldst thou beg, Laertes,   45
That shall not be my offer, not thy asking?
The head is not more native to the heart,
The hand more instrumental to the mouth,
Than is the throne of Denmark to thy father.
What wouldst thou have, Laertes?

    Laer.   My dread Lord,   50
Your leave and favour to return to France;
From whence though willingly I came to Denmark
To show my duty in your coronation,
Yet now, I must confess, that duty done,
My thoughts and wishes bend again toward France,   55
And bow them to your gracious leave and pardon.

    King.   Have you your father's leave?   What says
        Polonius?

    Pol.   'A hath, my lord, wrung from me my slow leave
By laboursome petition; and at last
Upon his will I seal'd my hard consent.   60
I do beseech you, give him leave to go.

    King.   Take thy fair hour, Laertes; time be thine,
And thy best graces spend it at thy will!
But now, my cousin Hamlet, and my son—

    Ham.   [*Aside.*]   A little more than kin, and less than
        kind.   65

    King.   How is it that the clouds still hang on you?

38. **delated:** detailed; set forth at length.
39. **let your haste . . . duty:** Let your haste demonstrate your sense of duty.

41. **nothing:** not at all.

44. **of reason:** reasonably. Claudius will refuse no reasonable request.
45. **thou:** The King changes from the formal *you* to the more familiar *thou*. Clearly, he favours Laertes, possibly because of affection, possibly because he is the son of Polonius, the Lord Chamberlain, whose approval of Claudius's actions so far must have been of influence on the court (see lines 14-16).
47. **native:** naturally related; closely akin to.

56. **pardon:** *permission* to depart, and also *forgiveness* (for wishing to leave so soon the court of such a king).

60. **Upon his will . . . consent:** to his desire I added my hard-won consent. Polonius, who delights in verbal quibbles, carries on the legal metaphor suggested by *petition* and *will*.
63. **thy best graces:** your very fine accomplishments and qualities.
64. **cousin:** can refer to almost any relationship in Elizabethan English. Here it means *nephew*.
65. **A little more . . . kind:** Hamlet's first line in the play, a quibble on words, is typical of him. **kind:** this could mean *natural* as well as *benevolent*, and was pronounced *kinn'd*. Thus Hamlet means that Claudius is related to him by being both uncle and stepfather, but is neither benevolent nor natural (because of his incestuous marriage to Gertrude).

Ham.   Not so, my lord; I am too much in the sun.
Queen.   Good Hamlet, cast thy nighted colour off,
And let thine eye look like a friend on Denmark.
Do not for ever with thy vailed lids   70
Seek for thy noble father in the dust.
Thou know'st 'tis common—all that lives must die,
Passing through nature to eternity.
  Ham.   Ay, madam, it is common.
  Queen.   If it be,
Why seems it so particular with thee?   75
  Ham.   Seems, madam! Nay, it is; I know not seems.
'Tis not alone my inky cloak, good mother,
Nor customary suits of solemn black,
Nor windy suspiration of forc'd breath,
No, nor the fruitful river in the eye,   80
Nor the dejected haviour of the visage,
Together with all forms, moods, shapes of grief,
That can denote me truly.   These, indeed, seem;
For they are actions that a man might play;
But I have that within which passes show—   85
These but the trappings and the suits of woe.
  King.   'Tis sweet and commendable in your nature,
          Hamlet,
To give these mourning duties to your father;
But you must know your father lost a father;
That father lost lost his; and the survivor bound,   90
In filial obligation, for some term
To do obsequious sorrow.   But to persever
In obstinate condolement is a course
Of impious stubbornness; 'tis unmanly grief;
It shows a will most incorrect to heaven,   95
A heart unfortified, a mind impatient,
An understanding simple and unschool'd;
For what we know must be, and is as common
As any the most vulgar thing to sense,
Why should we in our peevish opposition   .   100
Take it to heart?   Fie! 'tis a fault to heaven,
A fault against the dead, a fault to nature,

67. **too much in the sun:** Hamlet feels he is too much in the sun of court favour. (He wants to return to Wittenberg.) He is also too much a *son* to Claudius, who ought to be merely his uncle, and resents being called "son" in line 64. Dr Johnson has suggested that there is also a reference to the proverbial expression, "Out of God's blessing into the warm sun", which meant "to be out of house and home". This would be a hint that Hamlet is being deprived of his succession to the throne.

68. **nighted:** black as night.

70. **vailed:** downcast; lowered.

73. **nature:** life.

74. **common:** Hamlet is perhaps punning on the meaning "vulgar; disgusting".

75. **particular:** *special*, contrasted with *common* in line 72.

79. **suspiration:** sigh.

81. **haviour:** bearing; carriage. J. Dover Wilson suggests that in this bitter picture of "seeming" Hamlet is describing his mother's reactions to his father's death.

90. **That father lost:** that father who was lost.

91. **obsequious:** *funereal*; *pertaining to obsequies*, or perhaps *dutiful*.

93. **condolement:** grief; sorrow.

95. **incorrect:** unsubdued. Literally it means *uncorrected* and hence *unsubmissive*.

98-9. **as common ... sense:** as common and ordinary as the commonest thing we can perceive.

101. **to heaven:** against heaven.

To reason most absurd; whose common theme
Is death of fathers, and who still hath cried,
From the first corse till he that died to-day,   105
"This must be so". We pray you throw to earth
This unprevailing woe, and think of us
As of a father; for let the world take note
You are the most immediate to our throne;
And with no less nobility of love   110
Than that which dearest father bears his son
Do I impart toward you. For your intent
In going back to school in Wittenberg,
It is most retrograde to our desire;
And we beseech you bend you to remain   115
Here, in the cheer and comfort of our eye,
Our chiefest courtier, cousin, and our son.
   Queen. Let not thy mother lose her prayers, Hamlet:
I pray thee stay with us; go not to Wittenberg.
   Ham. I shall in all my best obey you, madam.   120
   King. Why, 'tis a loving and a fair reply.
Be as ourself in Denmark. Madam, come;
This gentle and unforc'd accord of Hamlet
Sits smiling to my heart; in grace whereof,
No jocund health that Denmark drinks to-day   125
But the great cannon to the clouds shall tell,
And the King's rouse the heaven shall bruit again,
Re-speaking earthly thunder. Come away.
                [Flourish. Exeunt, all but HAMLET.
   Ham. O, that this too too solid flesh would melt,
Thaw, and resolve itself into a dew!   130
Or that the Everlasting had not fix'd
His canon 'gainst self-slaughter! O God! God!
How weary, stale, flat, and unprofitable,
Seem to me all the uses of this world!
Fie on 't! Ah, fie! 'tis an unweeded garden,   135
That grows to seed; things rank and gross in nature
Possess it merely. That it should come to this!
But two months dead! Nay, not so much, not two.
So excellent a king that was to this

103. **whose**: *i.e.* reason's.

104. **still**: ever; continually.

105. **the first corse**: This was Abel, and it is ironic when we reflect that he was killed by his brother, Cain.

107. **unprevailing**: unavailing.

109. **the most immediate**: a bid for Hamlet's support for the new reign? Hamlet has already made his disapproval of Claudius quite clear by wearing mourning at this Council just after the King's marriage, and by his antagonistic remarks. The promise is referred to again at III. ii. 325.

112. **impart**: the construction is confused. Probably Claudius forgot he had used *with* in line 110, and treats the sentence as if *nobility* were the object.

113. **school**: university. Shakespeare was perhaps aware that Wittenberg was a favourite place of study with Danish students. Hamlet is to remain in Denmark because he is potentially dangerous to Claudius, who, having won the throne, is suspicious of similar ambitions in others.

114. **retrograde**: contrary.

115. **bend you**: incline yourself.

124. **in grace whereof**: in honour of which.

126. **the great cannon**: The Danes were noted for this custom, and the Danish Court for its heavy drinking, in Shakespeare's time. Claudius is certainly made to conform to the popular impression of the intemperate Danes.

127. **rouse**: revel; **draught**; drinking bruit again: sound again; re-echo.

129. **solid**: The early Quartos read *sallied*, which might mean *assailed* or might be a version of *sullied*. The latter is a particularly attractive possibility suggesting an image of snow, stained and unlovely.

130. **resolve**: dissolve. It was thought that there were four elements— air, earth, fire, and water—and that water predominated in the body. Thus Hamlet's wish is not so odd as it might seem to us.

132. **canon**: decree.

134. **uses**: habits and customs.

135. **an unweeded garden**: This image of weeds or diseased plants is used frequently in the play to suggest the "something rotten in the state of Denmark", and it is the more effective when we hear Laertes's warning to Ophelia, and remember her fate (see note I. iii. 40).

137. **merely**: wholly; utterly.

139. **to this**: compared with this.

135.4

Hyperion to a satyr; so loving to my mother,   140
That he might not beteem the winds of heaven
Visit her face too roughly.   Heaven and earth!
Must I remember?   Why, she would hang on him
As if increase of appetite had grown
By what it fed on; and yet, within a month—   145
Let me not think on 't.   Frailty, thy name is woman!—
A little month, or ere those shoes were old
With which she followed my poor father's body,
Like Niobe, all tears—why she, even she—
O God! a beast that wants discourse of reason   150
Would have mourn'd longer—married with my uncle,
My father's brother; but no more like my father
Than I to Hercules.   Within a month,
Ere yet the salt of most unrighteous tears
Had left the flushing in her galled eyes,   155
She married.   O, most wicked speed, to post
With such dexterity to incestuous sheets!
It is not, nor it cannot come to good.
But break, my heart, for I must hold my tongue.

Enter HORATIO, MARCELLUS, *and* BERNARDO.

  Hor.   Hail to your lordship!
  Ham.   I am glad to see you well. 160
Horatio—or do I forget myself.
  Hor.   The same, my lord, and your poor servant ever.
  Ham.   Sir, my good friend.   I 'll change that name with
    you.
And what make you from Wittenberg, Horatio?
Marcellus?   165
  Mar.   My good lord!
  Ham.   I am very glad to see you. [*To* BERNARDO.] Good
    even, sir.—
But what, in faith, make you from Wittenberg?
  Hor.   A truant disposition, good my lord.
  Ham.   I would not hear your enemy say so;   170
Nor shall you do my ear that violence,
To make it truster of your own report

140. **Hyperion:** A Titan, and father of Helios, the Sun-god, with whom he has often been confused, even in Homer. Helios was always represented as a very beautiful youth, with luxuriant golden curls. **Satyr:** a woodland god or demon in Greek mythology, part human, part beast.

141. **beteem:** allow; permit.

147. **or ere:** before.

149. **Niobe:** A queen whose six sons and six daughters were slain by Apollo and Artemis because she had insulted their mother, Leto. Zeus placed Niobe on the top of Mount Sipylos in Lydia and changed her into a stone whence tears of grief continued to flow.

150. **wants discourse of reason:** lacks the reasoning faculty.

154. **unrighteous:** because they were insincere.

155. **left . . . eyes:** ceased to redden her eyes which were sore with weeping. Possibly, however, *flushing* may be used in the common sense of *filling with water*.

157. **dexterity:** speed. **incestuous:** marriage with a deceased husband's brother was forbidden by both Roman Catholic and Anglican churches. It is important to note that already, before the Ghost reveals anything, Hamlet is suffering from a deep disgust and emotional disturbance due to this marriage of his mother's.

161. **Horatio . . . myself:** Hamlet at first does not recognise Horatio perhaps through preoccupation.

163. **change that name:** *i.e.* exchange the name of friend.

164. **what make you:** what are you doing.

Against yourself. I know you are no truant.
But what is your affair in Elsinore?
We 'll teach you to drink deep ere you depart.   175
   Hor. My lord, I came to see your father's funeral.
   Ham. I prithee do not mock me, fellow-student;
I think it was to see my mother's wedding.
   Hor. Indeed, my lord, it followed hard upon.
   Ham. Thrift, thrift, Horatio! The funeral bak'd-meats 180
Did coldly furnish forth the marriage tables.
Would I had met my dearest foe in heaven
Or ever I had seen that day, Horatio!
My father—methinks I see my father.
   Hor. Where, my lord?
   Ham.   In my mind's eye, Horatio,   185
   Hor. I saw him once; 'a was a goodly king.
   Ham. 'A was a man, take him for all in all,
I shall not look upon his like again.
   Hor. My lord, I think I saw him yesternight.
   Ham. Saw who?   190
   Hor. My lord, the King your father.
   Ham.   The King my father!
   Hor. Season your admiration for a while
With an attent ear, till I may deliver,
Upon the witness of these gentlemen,
This marvel to you.
   Ham.   For God's love, let me hear.   195
   Hor. Two nights together had these gentlemen,
Marcellus and Bernardo, on their watch,
In the dead waste and middle of the night,
Been thus encount'red. A figure like your father,
Armed at point exactly, cap-a-pe,   200
Appears before them, and with solemn march
Goes slow and stately by them; thrice he walk'd
By their oppress'd and fear-surprised eyes,
Within his truncheon's length; whilst they, distill'd
Almost to jelly with the act of fear,   205
Stand dumb and speak not to him. This to me
In dreadful secrecy impart they did;

175. **drink deep**: a bitter allusion by Hamlet to Claudius's carousing.

180. **bak'd-meats**: *i.e.* pastry of all kinds. The reference here is to the old custom of serving up a cold entertainment to the mourners at a funeral.

182. **dearest**: bitterest; deadliest; in Shakespeare, *dear* is used of anything which affects a person closely either for pleasure or grief, love or hatred.

185. **Where, my lord**: Horatio is startled, thinking the ghost has appeared to Hamlet.

186. **I saw him once**: Probably better punctuated with a dash before *once*. Horatio is about to blurt out his news, and then thinks better of it.

192. **Season your admiration**: temper or moderate your wonder.

193. **attent**: attentive. **deliver**: relate.

198. **dead waste**: the desolate hours, silent and lifeless as death.

200. **Armed at point exactly**: armed fully at all points. **cap-a-pe**: from head to foot.

204. **his truncheon's length**: The truncheon would be a field-marshal's baton, which the king, as commander of the Danish forces, would carry. **distill'd**: softened by melting.

205. **act**: operation; action.

And I with them the third night kept the watch;
Where, as they had delivered, both in time,
Form of the thing, each word made true and good,   210
The apparition comes. I knew your father;
These hands are not more like.
  Ham.   But where was this?
  Mar. My lord, upon the platform where we watch.
  Ham. Did you not speak to it?
  Hor.   My lord, I did;
But answer made it none; yet once methought   215
It lifted up it head and did address
Itself to motion, like as it would speak;
But even then the morning cock crew loud,
And at the sound it shrunk in haste away
And vanish'd from our sight.
  Ham.   'Tis very strange.   220
  Hor. As I do live, my honour'd lord, 'tis true;
And we did think it writ down in our duty
To let you know of it.
  Ham. Indeed, indeed, sirs, but this troubles me.
Hold you the watch to-night?
  All.   We do, my lord.   225
  Ham. Arm'd say you?
  All.   Arm'd, my lord.
  Ham. From top to toe?
  All.   My lord, from head to foot.
  Ham. Then saw you not his face?
  Hor. O yes, my lord; he wore his beaver up.
  Ham. What, look'd he frowningly?   230
  Hor. A countenance more in sorrow than in anger.
  Ham. Pale or red?
  Hor. Nay, very pale.
  Ham.   And fix'd his eyes upon you?
  Hor. Most constantly.
  Ham.   I would I had been there.
  Hor. It would have much amaz'd you.   235
  Ham. Very like, very like. Stay'd it long?

212. **These hands . . . like:** *i.e.* than the apparition and Hamlet's father.

226. **Arm'd:** This refers to the ghost, and not to the manner in which Marcellus and Bernardo are to keep watch.

229. **beaver:** the movable front part of the helmet, which could be pushed up or down.

230. **frowningly:** In I. i. 62, the ghost is described as frowning, yet here Horatio says it was sorrowful rather than angry.

235. **amaz'd:** struck with astonishment. The word was more forceful in Shakespeare's time than it is now.

Hor. While one with moderate haste might tell a hun-
 dred.
Both. Longer, longer.
Hor. Not when I saw 't.
Ham.   His beard was grizzl'd—no?
Hor. It was, as I have seen it in his life,   240
A sable silver'd.
Ham.   I will watch to-night;
Perchance 'twill walk again.
Hor.   I warr'nt it will.
Ham. If it assume my noble father's person,
I 'll speak to it, though hell itself should gape
And bid me hold my peace. I pray you all, 245
If you have hitherto conceal'd this sight,
Let it be tenable in your silence still;
And whatsomever else shall hap to-night,
Give it an understanding, but no tongue;
I will requite your loves. So, fare you well— 250
Upon the platform, 'twixt eleven and twelve,
I 'll visit you.
All.   Our duty to your honour.
Ham. Your loves, as mine to you; farewell.
         [*Exeunt all but* HAMLET.
My father's spirit in arms! All is not well.
I doubt some foul play. Would the night were come! 255
Till then sit still, my soul. Foul deeds will rise,
Though all the earth o'erwhelm them, to men's eyes. [*Exit.*

SCENE III. *Elsinore. The house of Polonius.*

Enter LAERTES *and* OPHELIA *his sister.*

Laer. My necessaries are embark'd. Farewell.
And, sister, as the winds give benefit
And convoy is assistant, do not sleep.
But let me hear from you.
Oph.   Do you doubt that?
Laer. For Hamlet, and the trifling of his favour, 5
Hold it a fashion and a toy in blood,

237. **tell**: count.

239. **grizzl'd**: grey.

247. **tenable**: kept; retained. **still**: ever; always.

253. **Your loves ... you**: Hamlet does not want their *duty* but their *love* as between friends, offering his own in return.

255. **doubt**: suspect.

ACT I. SCENE III

This domestic scene is another contrast with the previous two, and is skilfully placed to give a pause before introducing the Ghost again. It presents to us the family whose fate is so much bound up with that of Hamlet, and starts another train in the plot—Ophelia's rejection of Hamlet's love.

3. **convoy is assistant**: means of conveyance are available.

6. **fashion**: passing mood; something transient. **toy in blood**: a whim or caprice, dictated by passion or impulse.

A violet in the youth of primy nature,
Forward not permanent, sweet not lasting,
The perfume and suppliance of a minute;
No more.
  Oph. No more but so?
  Laer.   Think it no more;   10
For nature crescent does not grow alone
In thews and bulk, but as this temple waxes,
The inward service of the mind and soul
Grows wide withal. Perhaps he loves you now,
And now no soil nor cautel doth besmirch   15
The virtue of his will; but you must fear,
His greatness weigh'd, his will is not his own;
For he himself is subject to his birth:
He may not, as unvalued persons do,
Carve for himself; for on his choice depends   20
The sanity and health of this whole state;
And therefore must his choice be circumscrib'd
Unto the voice and yielding of that body
Whereof he is the head. Then if he says he loves you,
It fits your wisdom so far to believe it   25
As he in his particular act and place
May give his saying deed; which is no further
Than the main voice of Denmark goes withal.
Then weigh what loss your honour may sustain,
If with too credent ear you list his songs,   30
Or lose your heart, or your chaste treasure open
To his unmast'red importunity.
Fear it, Ophelia, fear it, my dear sister;
And keep you in the rear of your affection,
Out of the shot and danger of desire.   35
The chariest maid is prodigal enough
If she unmask her beauty to the moon.
Virtue itself scapes not calumnious strokes;
The canker galls the infants of the spring
Too oft before their buttons be disclos'd;   40
And in the morn and liquid dew of youth
Contagious blastments are most imminent.

7. **primy nature:** nature in its springtime.

9. **suppliance of a minute:** an amusement to fill up a vacant moment.

11. **crescent:** growing. **alone:** only.
12. **temple:** *i.e.* the body. The image is Scriptural, and suggests the word *service* in the next line. Laertes is warning Ophelia that as Hamlet grows, his awareness of his duties (*service*) will widen in scope, too.

15. **cautel:** deceit; craft.
16. **his will:** intentions.
17. **His greatness weigh'd:** when you consider his high position.

19. **unvalued:** worthless; of low rank.

23. **the voice and yielding:** the approval and consent.

26-7. **As he in his particular . . . deed:** She is to believe him only as far as his particular ability and rank permit him to fulfil his words.

30. **credent:** credulous. **list:** listen to.

34. **keep you . . . affection:** Do not let your love run away with you.
36. **chariest:** most scrupulous, careful, or modest.
39. **canker:** the canker-worm.
40. **buttons:** buds. **disclos'd:** unclosed; opened. This image is to be developed later. Here, Ophelia is already associated with flowers ("violet" in line 7, "primrose" line 50) and her own sweetness and virtue likened to a bud. In IV. v, at IV. vii. 167-76, and in V. i, where she is "allow'd her virgin crants", Laertes hopes violets will grow from her grave and the Queen casts flowers on her grave (lines 233-6), we find the association deepening. Laertes's warning of "contagious blastments" is almost prophetic, for we know that Denmark is "an unweeded garden", where a delicate plant will easily succumb.
42. **blastments:** blighting influences.

Be wary, then; best safety lies in fear:
Youth to itself rebels, though none else near.
    Oph.   I shall the effect of this good lesson keep   45
As watchman to my heart.   But, good my brother,
Do not, as some ungracious pastors do,
Show me the steep and thorny way to heaven,
Whiles, like a puff'd and reckless libertine,
Himself the primrose path of dalliance treads   50
And recks not his own rede.
    Laer.   O, fear me not!

Enter POLONIUS.

I stay too long.   But here my father comes.
A double blessing is a double grace;
Occasion smiles upon a second leave.
    Pol.   Yet here, Laertes!   Aboard, aboard, for shame!   55
The wind sits in the shoulder of your sail,
And you are stay'd for.   There—my blessing with thee!
And these few precepts in thy memory
Look thou character.   Give thy thoughts no tongue,
Nor any unproportion'd thought his act.   60
Be thou familiar, but by no means vulgar.
Those friends thou hast, and their adoption tried,
Grapple them to thy soul with hoops of steel;
But do not dull thy palm with entertainment
Of each new-hatch'd, unfledg'd courage.   Beware   65
Of entrance to a quarrel; but, being in,
Bear't that th' opposed may beware of thee.
Give every man thy ear, but few thy voice;
Take each man's censure, but reserve thy judgment.
Costly thy habit as thy purse can buy,   70
But not express'd in fancy; rich, not gaudy;
For the apparel oft proclaims the man;
And they in France of the best rank and station
Are of a most select and generous choice in that.
Neither a borrower nor a lender be;   75
For loan oft loses both itself and friend,
And borrowing dulls the edge of husbandry.

47. **ungracious pastors:** graceless priests.

49. **puff'd:** bloated.
50. **primrose path:** *i.e.* the path strewn with primroses and so, attractive.
51. **recks not his own rede:** Takes no heed of his own advice. **me:** for me.

54. **Occasion smiles . . . leave:** This provides a happy opportunity of a second leave-taking.

58. **precepts:** For some of the maxims in the following lines, Shakespeare was indebted to Lyly's *Euphues*, as may be seen from the following extracts: "Be not lavish of thy tongue". "Be not quarrelous on every light occasion: they never fight without provoking (*i.e.* provocation) and once provoked they never cease." "It shall be there better to hear what they say than to speak what thou thinkest." Another parallel has been found in the ten "admirable precepts of worldly prudence" left by Lord Burghley to his son. Shakespeare clearly intended Polonius's speech to be typical of a father's worldly advice to his son. Yet, admirable though the sentiments appear, they are uttered with such smugness, and motivated so obviously by the desire for personal gain, that we can only despise Polonius for them. They are typical of the outwardly fine, but inwardly rotten, court that so disgusts Hamlet.
59. **character:** inscribe, write.
60. **unproportion'd:** unsuitable; not befitting the occasion. **his:** its.
61. **Be thou familiar . . . vulgar:** Be friendly, but do not make yourself too cheap.
62. **and their adoption tried:** when you have tried those friends you have adopted.
64. **dull thy palm:** make your hand coarse, and so unfeeling and unable to discriminate. The image is of shaking hands so frequently that the palm becomes hard and callous.
65. **courage:** adventurer; daredevil.
69. **censure:** opinion; judgment (not necessarily unfavourable).
74. **choice:** This is an emendation from the *chief* of the Quartos and the first Folio. All editors agree that the text is corrupt, some defending the reading, "Are most select and generous, chief (i.e. *mainly*) in that", which omits *of a.* **generous:** *i.e.* show their good breeding.
77. **husbandry:** thrift; economy.

This above all—to thine own self be true,
And it must follow, as the night the day,
Thou canst not then be false to any man.   80
Farewell; my blessing season this in thee!
    Laer. Most humbly do I take my leave, my lord.
    Pol. The time invites you; go, your servants tend.
    Laer. Farewell, Ophelia; and remember well
What I have said to you.
    Oph.   'Tis in my memory lock'd,   85
And you yourself shall keep the key of it.
    Laer. Farewell.   [*Exit.*
    Pol. What is 't, Ophelia, he hath said to you?
    Oph. So please you, something touching the Lord Ham-
    let.
    Pol. Marry, well bethought!   90
'Tis told me he hath very oft of late
Given private time to you; and you yourself
Have of your audience been most free and bounteous.
If it be so—as so 'tis put on me,
And that in way of caution—I must tell you   95
You do not understand yourself so clearly
As it behoves my daughter and your honour.
What is between you? Give me up the truth.
    Oph. He hath, my lord, of late made many tenders
Of his affection to me.   100
    Pol. Affection! Pooh! You speak like a green girl,
Unsifted in such perilous circumstance.
Do you believe his tenders, as you call them?
    Oph. I do not know, my lord, what I should think.
    Pol. Marry, I will teach you: think yourself a baby   105
That you have ta'en these tenders for true pay
Which are not sterling. Tender yourself more dearly;
Or—not to crack the wind of the poor phrase,
Running it thus—you 'll tender me a fool.
    Oph. My lord, he hath importun'd me with love   110
In honourable fashion.
    Pol. Ay, fashion you may call it; go to, go to.
    Oph. And hath given countenance to his speech, my lord,

81. **season:** mature; ripen. Polonius hopes that the seeds of wisdom he has sown in Laertes's mind will be helped to fruition by his blessing.
83. **tend:** attend.

93. **bounteous:** Polonius uses the pompous court word *audience* for an interview. He means that Ophelia has been too ready to see Hamlet.
94. **put on me:** impressed on me.

102. **Unsifted:** inexperienced.

107. **sterling:** valuable; of solid worth. **Tender . . . dearly:** take more care of yourself.
108-9. **crack the wind . . . Running:** The image is of hounds being run after a hare.
109. **tender me a fool:** Here Polonius again uses *tender* with the meaning *offer*. He may mean that Ophelia will appear a fool but since *fool* can also be applied to a baby, he is probably saying that she will present him with a child.
112. **fashion:** Polonius is again playing on Ophelia's words, giving *fashion* the sense Laertes gives it in line 6. **go to:** an expression of impatience.

With almost all the holy vows of heaven.

  Pol. Ay, springes to catch woodcocks! I do know,   115
When the blood burns, how prodigal the soul
Lends the tongue vows. These blazes, daughter,
Giving more light than heat—extinct in both,
Even in their promise, as it is a-making—
You must not take for fire. From this time   120
Be something scanter of your maiden presence;
Set your entreatments at a higher rate
Than a command to parle. For Lord Hamlet,
Believe so much in him, that he is young,
And with a larger tether may he walk   125
Than may be given you. In few, Ophelia,
Do not believe his vows; for they are brokers,
Not of that dye which their investments show,
But mere implorators of unholy suits,
Breathing like sanctified and pious bonds,   130
The better to beguile. This is for all—
I would not, in plain terms, from this time forth
Have you so slander any moment leisure
As to give words or talk with the Lord Hamlet.
Look to 't, I charge you. Come your ways.   135
  Oph. I shall obey, my lord.   [*Exeunt.*

SCENE IV. *Elsinore. The guard-platform of the Castle.*

Enter HAMLET, HORATIO, *and* MARCELLUS.

  Ham. The air bites shrewdly; it is very cold.
  Hor. It is a nipping and an eager air.
  Ham. What hour now?
  Hor.   I think it lacks of twelve.
  Mar. No, it is struck.
  Hor. Indeed? I heard it not. It then draws near the
      season   5
Wherein the spirit held his wont to walk.
        [*A flourish of trumpets, and two pieces go off.*
What does this mean, my lord?
  Ham. The King doth wake to-night and takes his rouse,

115. **springes:** snares. Woodcocks were easily caught in snares, and so were considered stupid. Hence a woodcock was a simpleton.

116. **prodigal:** prodigally.

118-9. **extinct in both ... a-making:** both of which (heat and light) are extinguished just as they are being kindled and promise to come to something.

121. **something scanter:** rather more sparing.

122. **entreatments:** interviews; conversations.

125. **larger tether:** Hamlet has more freedom than can be allowed a young girl such as Ophelia.

127. **brokers:** middle-men; agents. Polonius implies *pandar* or *go-between.* The word could also be used of a second-hand clothes dealer.

128. **dye:** colour; *i.e.* character. **investments:** vesture; dress. He puns this time on the sense of *money investments,* which was suggested by *brokers.*

129. **implorators:** implorers; pleaders. **suits:** *requests,* but again quibbling with the sense of *clothing* after *investments* and *brokers.*

130. **Breathing:** speaking. **bonds:** legal documents, or contracts, which are often headed with religious formulae. The idea probably derives from *brokers* and *investments,* though some editors think **pious bonds** are marriage vows. In any case, Hamlet's declarations are tricked out in finery, pretending to holiness, in order to deceive. The pun on clothing is still present in the suggestion of a clergyman's *bands.*

133. **slander any moment leisure:** disgrace, or perhaps misuse, any moment of leisure.

135. **Come your ways:** come along.

ACT I. SCENE IV

2. **eager:** sharp; biting.

8. **wake:** hold a late revel. **rouse:** draught.

Keeps wassail, and the swagg'ring up-spring reels,
And, as he drains his draughts of Rhenish down,   10
The kettle-drum and trumpet thus bray out
The triumph of his pledge.
    Hor.   Is it a custom?
    Ham. Ay, marry, is 't;
But to my mind, though I am native here
And to the manner born, it is a custom   15
More honour'd in the breach than the observance.
This heavy-headed revel east and west
Makes us traduc'd and tax'd of other nations;
They clepe us drunkards, and with swinish phrase
Soil our addition; and, indeed, it takes   20
From our achievements, though perform'd at height,
The pith and marrow of our attribute.
So, oft it chances in particular men
That, for some vicious mole of nature in them,
As in their birth, wherein they are not guilty,   25
Since nature cannot choose his origin;
By the o'ergrowth of some complexion,
Oft breaking down the pales and forts of reason;
Or by some habit that too much o'er-leavens
The form of plausive manners—that these men,   30
Carrying, I say, the stamp of one defect,
Being nature's livery or fortune's star,
His virtues else, be they as pure as grace,
As infinite as man may undergo,
Shall in the general censure take corruption   35
From that particular fault. The dram of eale
Doth all the noble substance of a doubt
To his own scandal.

                Enter GHOST.

    Hor.   Look, my lord, it comes.
    Ham. Angels and ministers of grace defend us!
Be thou a spirit of health or goblin damn'd,   40
Bring with thee airs from heaven or blasts from hell,
Be thy intents wicked or charitable,

9. **wassail:** carousing; revelry. **up-spring reels:** dances (rather drunkenly) the up-spring, a kind of wild dance with which old German celebrations ended.

16. **More honour'd . . . observance:** It would be more honourable for it to be neglected instead of observed.

18. **tax'd of:** censured by.

19. **clepe:** call.

20. **addition:** *title* (with the idea here of *reputation*), or *the sum total of our qualities.* See Introduction, p. 19.

21. **at height:** with the utmost (skill or courage).

22. **attribute:** reputation; honour (or *talents*).

23. **particular:** certain; individual.

24. **mole of nature:** natural blemish of character (or *feature*).

25. **As:** such as.

26. **his:** its.

27-8. **By the o'ergrowth . . . reason:** Medieval theories of physiology held that the body was made up of four humours, and a man might be melancholy, phlegmatic, sanguine, or choleric, depending on which of the four predominated in his particular *complexion* or mixture. Madness was caused by the *o'ergrowth* of one of these humours, usually melancholy. It is worth noting that some critics see Hamlet as an example of melancholy madness. **complexion,** however, can also mean the *natural colour of the skin.*

29. **o'er-leavens:** permeates and modifies. The image is of dough being fermented.

30. **plausive:** pleasing.

32. **nature's livery:** a natural blemish. (*Livery:* distinctive dress or badge worn by a person's servants.) **fortune's star:** a blemish of character given by fortune, through the influence of the planets. *Star* here refers to astrological influences.

33. **His virtues else:** his other virtues.

34. **undergo:** experience.

35. **in the general censure:** in the opinion of most men.

36-8. **The dram of eale . . . scandal:** A passage whose general meaning is quite clear, but about whose precise form there has been much controversy. **eale:** most probably *evil* (in both Quartos, we find *deale* for *devil* in II. ii. 583), and so the general sense is that a small quantity of evil taints a man's noble qualities so completely in the eyes of others that his reputation is ruined. The most convincing emendation to make this quite clear would be *often dout* (**dout:** extinguish) for **of a doubt,** though this has to fight for acceptance with some fifty others.

38. **Look, my Lord:** Again the Ghost surprises us, lulled into forgetfulness by Hamlet's speech, though we had been expecting it.

40. **spirit of health:** a good spirit, of beneficent influence.

Thou com'st in such a questionable shape
That I will speak to thee. I 'll call thee Hamlet,
King, father, royal Dane. O, answer me!   45
Let me not burst in ignorance, but tell
Why thy canoniz'd bones, hearsed in death,
Have burst their cerements; why the sepulchre
Wherein we saw thee quietly enurn'd
Hath op'd his ponderous and marble jaws   50
To cast thee up again. What may this mean
That thou, dead corse, again in complete steel
Revisits thus the glimpses of the moon,
Making night hideous, and we fools of nature
So horridly to shake our disposition   55
With thoughts beyond the reaches of our souls?
Say, why is this? wherefore? What should we do?
                              [GHOST *beckons* HAMLET.
   Hor. It beckons you to go away with it,
As if it some impartment did desire
To you alone.
   Mar.   Look with what courteous action   60
It waves you to a more removed ground.
But do not go with it.
   Hor.   No, by no means.
   Ham. It will not speak; then I will follow it.
   Hor. Do not, my lord.
   Ham.   Why, what should be the fear?
I do not set my life at a pin's fee;   65
And for my soul, what can it do to that,
Being a thing immortal as itself?
It waves me forth again; I 'll follow it.
   Hor. What if it tempt you toward the flood, my lord,
Or to the dreadful summit of the cliff   70
That beetles o'er his base into the sea,
And there assume some other horrible form,
Which might deprive your sovereignty of reason
And draw you into madness? Think of it:
The very place puts toys of desperation,   75
Without more motive, into every brain

43. **questionable**: *inviting question*, but also *doubtful, uncertain*.

47. **canoniz'd**: consecrated (by the burial service).

49. **enurn'd**: entombed.

54. **we fools of nature**: us human fools; *i.e.* they are fools when faced with the *supernatural*, being themselves of the *natural* world.
55. **disposition**: *normal temperament*, and so here probably *composure*.

59. **impartment**: communication.

61. **removed**: remote.

71. **his**: its.

73. **deprive your sovereignty of reason**: dethrone your reason.

75. **toys of desperation**: desperate, suicidal fancies or impulses.

That looks so many fathoms to the sea
And hears it roar beneath.
   Ham.   It waves me still.
Go on; 1 'll follow thee.
   Mar.   You shall not go, my lord.
   Ham.   Hold off your hands. 8o
   Hor.   Be rul'd; you shall not go.
   Ham.   My fate cries out,
And makes each petty arture in this body
As hardy as the Nemean lion's nerve.   [GHOST *beckons.*
Still am I call'd. Unhand me, gentlemen.
By heaven, I 'll make a ghost of him that lets me.   85
I say, away! Go on; I 'll follow thee.
                    [*Exeunt* GHOST *and* HAMLET.
   Hor.   He waxes desperate with imagination.
   Mar.   Let 's follow; 'tis not fit thus to obey him.
   Hor.   Have after. To what issue will this come?
   Mar.   Something is rotten in the state of Denmark.   90
   Hor.   Heaven will direct it.
   Mar.   Nay, let 's follow him.
                          [*Exeunt.*

   SCENE V. *Elsinore. The battlements of the Castle.*

              Enter GHOST *and* HAMLET.

   Ham.   Whither wilt thou lead me? Speak. I 'll go no
       further.
   Ghost.   Mark me.
   Ham.   I will.
   Ghost.   My hour is almost come,
When I to sulph'rous and tormenting flames
Must render up myself.
   Ham.   Alas, poor ghost!
   Ghost.   Pity me not, but lend thy serious hearing   5
To what I shall unfold.
   Ham.   Speak; I am bound to hear.
   Ghost.   So art thou to revenge, when thou shalt hear.
   Ham.   What?

82. **petty arture:** small ligament.

83. **hardy:** brave; bold. **Nemean lion's nerve:** The lion at Nemea was unharmed by darts of any kind. It was Hercules's first labour to destroy it. **nerve:** tendon; sinew.

85. **lets:** hinders.

89. **Have after:** After him!

91. **Nay:** *i.e.* Don't stop to talk.

ACT I. SCENE V

1. **Whither wilt thou lead me:** This obviously follows shortly after the "Go on: I 'll follow thee", of the previous scene, and indicates that the action proceeds without a pause.

6. **bound:** ready (cp. *homeward bound*, where again bound has no connection with *bind*). The ghost, however, in the following line, takes the word as connected with the latter in the sense of *under an obligation*.

Ghost. I am thy father's spirit,
Doom'd for a certain term to walk the night,   10
And for the day confin'd to fast in fires,
Till the foul crimes done in my days of nature
Are burnt and purg'd away. But that I am forbid
To tell the secrets of my prison-house,
I could a tale unfold whose lightest word   15
Would harrow up thy soul, freeze thy young blood,
Make thy two eyes, like stars, start from their spheres,
Thy knotted and combined locks to part,
And each particular hair to stand an end,
Like quills upon the fretful porpentine.   20
But this eternal blazon must not be
To ears of flesh and blood. List, list, O, list!
If thou didst ever thy dear father love—
    Ham. O God!
    Ghost. Revenge his foul and most unnatural murder.   25
    Ham. Murder!
    Ghost. Murder most foul, as in the best it is;
But this most foul, strange, and unnatural.
    Ham. Haste me to know 't, that I, with wings as swift
As meditation or the thoughts of love,   30
May sweep to my revenge.
    Ghost.   I find thee apt;
And duller shouldst thou be than the fat weed
That roots itself in ease on Lethe wharf,
Wouldst thou not stir in this. Now, Hamlet, hear:
'Tis given out that, sleeping in my orchard,   35
A serpent stung me; so the whole ear of Denmark
Is by a forged process of my death
Rankly abus'd; but know, thou noble youth,
The serpent that did sting thy father's life
Now wears his crown.
    Ham.   O my prophetic soul!   40
My uncle!
    Ghost. Ay, that incestuous, that adulterate beast,
With witchcraft of his wits, with traitorous gifts—
O wicked wit and gifts that have the power

11. **to fast**: fasting was considered the torment prescribed for the intemperate.   Chaucer tells us in *The Parson's Tale*, "the misese of helle shal been in defaut of mete and drinke".   This phrase suggests to some editors that Claudius, with his "heavy-headed revel" is merely following his brother's example, but it is doubtful that Shakespeare meant us to catch this implication.

12. **days of nature**: natural life.

17. **like stars . . . spheres**: Astrologers used the Ptolemaic theory that the sun, moon, planets, and stars were fixed in a series of concentric hollow spheres, by the motion of which they revolved round the earth as centre.   If a planet were to break away from its sphere, there would be calamitous disaster on earth.

19. **an**: on.

20. **porpentine**: porcupine.

21. **eternal blazon**: proclamation of the mysteries of eternity.   Sometimes, Shakespeare uses *eternal* as if with the sense of *infernal*, e.g. *Othello*, IV. ii. 130, "Some eternal villain", but it is hardly necessary to read such a meaning here.

27. **in the best**: at best.

32. **fat weed**: no allusion to any particular plant is meant.

33. **Lethe wharf**: the bank of the Lethe, the river of forgetfulness in the Lower World, which produced complete oblivion in all who drank of it.

35. **orchard**: garden.

37. **forged process**: falsified account.

38. **Rankly abus'd**: grossly deceived.

40. **prophetic soul**: Hamlet clearly suspected something, but exactly what, we cannot know, nor whether his suspicions involved Claudius. Earlier, he told us, "I doubt some foul play" (I. ii. 255).

42. **adulterate**: This word was used of almost any sexual immorality, so that it is not necessarily evidence of infidelity by Gertrude *before* her husband's death.   It might be referring to the crime of *incest* which so troubles Hamlet.

So to seduce!—won to his shameful lust   45
The will of my most seeming virtuous queen.
O Hamlet, what a falling off was there,
From me, whose love was of that dignity
That it went hand in hand even with the vow
I made to her in marriage; and to decline   50
Upon a wretch whose natural gifts were poor
To those of mine!
But virtue, as it never will be moved,
Though lewdness court it in a shape of heaven,
So lust, though to a radiant angel link'd,   55
Will sate itself in a celestial bed
And prey on garbage.
But soft! methinks I scent the morning air.
Brief let me be. Sleeping within my orchard,
My custom always of the afternoon,   60
Upon my secure hour thy uncle stole,
With juice of cursed hebona in a vial,
And in the porches of my ears did pour
The leperous distilment; whose effect
Holds such an enmity with blood of man   65
That swift as quicksilver it courses through
The natural gates and alleys of the body;
And with a sudden vigour it doth posset
And curd, like eager droppings into milk,
The thin and wholesome blood. So did it mine;   70
And a most instant tetter bark'd about,
Most lazar-like, with vile and loathsome crust,
All my smooth body.
Thus was I, sleeping, by a brother's hand
Of life, of crown, of queen, at once dispatch'd;   75
Cut off even in the blossoms of my sin,
Unhous'led, disappointed, unanel'd;
No reck'ning made, but sent to my account
With all my imperfections on my head.
O, horrible! O, horrible! most horrible!   80
If thou hast nature in thee, bear it not;
Let not the royal bed of Denmark be

49. **even with:** level with.
50. **decline Upon:** lower herself to.

54. **a shape of heaven:** a heavenly appearance or guise.
55-7. **lust ... garbage:** lust, though married to an angel, will glut itself and tire of even such a heavenly union, and turn away to prey on garbage.

61. **secure:** careless; unsuspecting.
62. **hebona:** Shakespeare possibly has in mind *henbane,* whose oil, according to a translation of Pliny (by Holland, 1601), "if it be but dropped into the eares is enough to trouble the brain". The word itself, however, is probably from Marlowe's "juice of hebon" (*Jew of Malta,* III. iv), which itself comes from Gower ("hebenus, that sleepy tree") who is referring not to the tree's poisonous properties, but to a description by Ovid of the God of Sleep's chamber panelled with *ebony.*
64. **leperous distilment:** distillation causing leprosy.

68. **posset:** curdle; coagulate.
69. **eager:** sharp; bitter. The image is of milk being curdled by the addition of ale or wine.
70. **wholesome:** healthy.
71-3. **a most instant tetter body:** an instantaneous eruption formed on my smooth skin like the bark round a tree. **lazar-like:** leper-like.

75. **dispatch'd:** deprived.

77. **Unhous'led:** without having received the Eucharist. **disappointed:** unprepared. **unanel'd:** without extreme unction.

81. **nature:** *i.e.* natural feeling.

A couch for luxury and damned incest.
But, howsomever thou pursuest this act,
Taint not thy mind, nor let thy soul contrive   85
Against thy mother aught; leave her to heaven,
And to those thorns that in her bosom lodge
To prick and sting her. Fare thee well at once.
The glowworm shows the matin to be near,
And gins to pale his uneffectual fire.   90
Adieu, adieu, adieu! Remember me.   [*Exit.*

   Ham. O all you host of heaven! O earth! What else?
And shall I couple hell?   O, fie! Hold, hold, my heart;
And you, my sinews, grow not instant old,
But bear me stiffly up. Remember thee!   95
Ay, thou poor ghost, whiles memory holds a seat
In this distracted globe. Remember thee!
Yea, from the table of my memory
I 'll wipe away all trivial fond records,
All saws of books, all forms, all pressures past,   100
That youth and observation copied there,
And thy commandment all alone shall live
Within the book and volume of my brain,
Unmix'd with baser matter. Yes, by heaven!
O most pernicious woman!   105
O villain, villain, smiling, damned villain!
My tables—meet it is I set it down
That one may smile, and smile, and be a villain;
At least I am sure it may be so in Denmark.   [*Writing.*
So, uncle, there you are. Now to my word: 110
It is "Adieu, adieu! Remember me".
I have sworn 't.

   Hor. [*Within.*] My lord, my lord!

Enter HORATIO *and* MARCELLUS.

Mar.   Lord Hamlet!
Hor.   Heavens secure him!
Ham.   So be it!
Mar.   Illo, ho, ho, my lord!   115
Ham.   Hillo, ho, ho, boy! Come, bird, come.

83. **luxury:** lust.

85-6. **nor let thy soul . . . aught:** Some would say that this complicates Hamlet's task, and is a reason for delay. Hamlet, however, never sees it as an obstacle. He does not mention it, for example, in the "prayer scene" (III. iii).

89. **matin:** morning.
90. **uneffectual:** useless because lost in morning light, or perhaps because burning without heat.

94. **instant:** instantly.

97. **distracted globe:** his head.
98. **table:** tablet. All this speech refers to the fashion of carrying a notebook. Here it is an image for Hamlet's brain.
99. **fond:** foolish.
100. **all forms, all pressures:** all sketches and impressions.

107. **My tables:** Here Hamlet actually takes out his own notebook. He has obviously been under immense strain, and can scarcely face the thoughts which the Ghost has left with him. This explains Hamlet's almost hysterical conduct in the lines that follow, and his ineffectual attempt here to control his mind. He is not pretending, for he has no motive, and why should he do so for the benefit of men to whom he will reveal his intention to feign madness?
110. **word:** motto, or watchword.

116. **Hillo, ho, ho, boy:** a falconer's call, with which Hamlet replies in mockery to Marcellus's cry.

Mar.   How is 't, my noble lord?

Hor.   What news, my lord?

Ham.   O, wonderful!

Hor.   Good my lord, tell it.

Ham.   No; you will reveal it.

Hor.   Not I, my lord, by heaven!

Mar.   Nor I, my lord.   120

Ham.   How say you, then; would heart of man once think
        it?
But you 'll be secret?

Both.   Ay, by heaven, my lord!

Ham.   There 's never a villain dwelling in all Denmark
But he 's an arrant knave.

Hor.   There needs no ghost, my lord, come from the
        grave   125
To tell us this.

Ham.   Why, right; you are in the right;
And so, without more circumstance at all,
I hold it fit that we shake hands and part;
You, as your business and desire shall point you—
For every man hath business and desire,   130
Such as it is; and for my own poor part,
Look you, I will go pray.

Hor.   These are but wild and whirling words, my lord.

Ham.   I am sorry they offend you, heartily; Yes, faith,
        heartily.

Hor.   There 's no offence, my lord.   135

Ham.   Yes, by Saint Patrick, but there is, Horatio,
And much offence too.   Touching this vision here—
It is an honest ghost, that let me tell you.
For your desire to know what is between us,
O'ermaster 't as you may.   And now, good friends,   140
As you are friends, scholars, and soldiers,
Give me one poor request.

Hor.   What is 't, my lord?   We will.

Ham.   Never make known what you have seen to-night.

Both.   My lord, we will not.

Ham.   Nay, but swear 't.

123-4. **There 's never ... knave:** Hamlet may have been about to confide in his listeners by saying "There is not a villain in Denmark as great as my uncle", but suddenly changes his mind and ends jestingly instead. He may, however, have been playing with them from the first.

127. **circumstance:** circumlocution.

136-42. **These lines,** Dover Wilson suggests, are an aside to Horatio. Marcellus, however, must be kept in the dark, and made to reveal nothing of what he already knows, so Hamlet swears them both to secrecy, intending to tell Horatio of the Ghost's revelations at the first suitable opportunity.

136. **Saint Patrick:** Various attempts have been made to explain why Hamlet should swear by this particular saint. He was keeper of Purgatory (whence the Ghost had come), and he is "patron saint of all blunders and confusion".

137. **much offence:** Hamlet takes up Horatio's word *offence*, using it in the sense of *crime*.

138. **honest ghost:** an honourable ghost, *i.e.* not a devil. It is only later that Hamlet says he has doubts (II. ii. 582-3). when he is trying to explain his delay,

Hor.   In faith, 145
My lord, not I.
    Mar.   Nor I, my lord, in faith.
    Ham. Upon my sword.
    Mar. We have sworn, my lord, already.
    Ham. Indeed, upon my sword, indeed.
    Ghost. [*Cries under the stage.*]   Swear.
    Ham. Ha, ha, boy! say'st thou so? Art thou there, true-
        penny?   150
Come on. You hear this fellow in the cellarage:
Consent to swear.
    Hor.   Propose the oath, my lord.
    Ham. Never to speak of this that you have seen,
Swear by my sword.
    Ghost. [*Beneath.*] Swear.   155
    Ham. Hic et ubique? Then we 'll shift our ground.
Come hither, gentlemen,
And lay your hands again upon my sword.
Swear by my sword
Never to speak of this that you have heard.   160
    Ghost. [*Beneath.*] Swear, by his sword.
    Ham. Well said, old mole! Canst work i' th' earth so
        fast?
A worthy pioneer! Once more remove, good friends.
    Hor. O day and night, but this is wondrous strange!
    Ham. And therefore as a stranger give it welcome.   165
There are more things in heaven and earth, Horatio,
Than are dreamt of in your philosophy.
But come.
Here, as before, never, so help you mercy,
How strange or odd some'er I bear myself—   170
As I perchance hereafter shall think meet
To put an antic disposition on—
That you, at such times, seeing me, never shall,
With arms encumb'red thus, or this head-shake,
Or by pronouncing of some doubtful phrase,   175
As "Well, well, we know" or "We could, an if we would"
Or "If we list to speak" or "There be, an if they might"

146. **not I**: the words do not refer to *swear*, but simply repeat the *will not* of line 145.

147. **Upon my sword**: *i.e.* on the hilt, which had the form of a cross.

150. **truepenny**: honest fellow.

156. **Hic et ubique**: here and everywhere. The use of Latin, and Hamlet's use of such terms as *truepenny*, *old mole*, *pioneer*, and the moving from one place to another, would all overawe Marcellus with the impression that Hamlet is a conjurer of spirits. He also swears a powerful *threefold* oath—not to speak of what he has seen, of what he has heard, or of the cause of Hamlet's "antic disposition".

163. **pioneer**: digger; miner.

167. **your**: The word is used to generalise. Hamlet does not mean Horatio's philosophy, but human philosophy in general. **philosophy**: science as understood by the Elizabethans.

172. **antic**: fantastic.

174. **encumb'red**: folded.

176. **an if we would**: if we wished.

177. **There be, an if they might**: There are some who could tell, if they were allowed.

Or such ambiguous giving out, to note
That you know aught of me—this do swear,
So grace and mercy at your most need help you.   180
   Ghost. [*Beneath.*] Swear.
   Ham.   Rest, rest, perturbed spirit! So, gentlemen,
With all my love I do commend me to you;
And what so poor a man as Hamlet is
May do t' express his love and friending to you,   185
God willing, shall not lack.   Let us go in together;
And still your fingers on your lips, I pray.
The time is out of joint.   O cursed spite,
That ever I was born to set it right!
Nay, come let 's go together.   [*Exeunt.*

178. **giving out**: intimations; hints.

185. **friending**: friendship.

ACT II

SCENE I. *Elsinore. The house of Polonius.*

Enter POLONIUS *and* REYNALDO.

Pol. Give him this money and these notes, Reynaldo.
Rey. I will, my lord.
Pol. You shall do marvellous wisely, good Reynaldo,
Before you visit him, to make inquire
Of his behaviour.
    Rey.   My lord, I did intend it.   5
Pol. Marry, well said; very well said. Look you, sir,
Enquire me first what Danskers are in Paris;
And how, and who, what means, and where they keep,
What company, at what expense; and finding
By this encompassment and drift of question   10
That they do know my son, come you more nearer
Than your particular demands will touch it.
Take you, as 'twere, some distant knowledge of him;
As thus; "I know his father and his friends,
And in part him". Do you mark this, Reynaldo?   15
    Rey. Ay, very well, my lord.
Pol. "And in part him—but" you may say "not well;
But if 't be he I mean, he 's very wild;
Addicted so and so"; and there put on him
What forgeries you please; marry, none so rank   20
As may dishonour him; take heed of that;
But, sir, such wanton, wild, and usual slips
As are companions noted and most known
To youth and liberty.
    Rey.   As gaming, my lord.
Pol. Ay, or drinking, fencing, swearing, quarrelling,   25
Drabbing—you may go so far.
    Rey. My lord, that would dishonour him.
Pol. Faith, no; as you may season it in the charge.
You must not put another scandal on him,

ACT II. SCENE I

1. **Give him this money:** That Laertes has sent for more money tells us that some time has passed since he left the Danish court for Paris. In fact it is more than two months, if we remember that in I. ii. 138 Hamlet said that his father had not been dead two months, and that in III. ii. 119 Ophelia remarks that the late king has been dead "twice two months". Act III takes place on the day after Act II (see II. ii. 517 and 521).

4. **inquire:** inquiry.

7. **Enquire me:** enquire for me. **Danskers:** Danes.
8. **keep:** live; reside.

10. **encompassment . . . questions:** circumventions and roundabout questions.
11-12. **come . . . touch it:** Instead of asking pointed direct questions, which might cause the person questioned to be silent or to lie, Reynaldo is to get nearer to the truth by Polonius's roundabout methods.
13. **Take you:** assume; pretend.

19-20. **put on him . . . please:** make whatever false accusations against him you please. **rank:** gross; excessive.

25. **fencing:** professional fencers were of ill-repute in Elizabethan times. (Claudius does not regard the art very highly—IV. vii. 74-7.)
26. **Drabbing:** associating with loose women.
28. **Faith, no:** So much for Polonius's advice to Laertes when they parted! This moral laxity, together with the hypocritical desire for respectability, are what disgust Hamlet so much about the Court in general and Polonius in particular. They are not the cause of his disillusionment, but they help to feed it, and intensify his loneliness. **season:** temper; modify.

79

That he is open to incontinency;   30
That 's not my meaning. But breathe his faults so quaintly
That they may seem the taints of liberty;
The flash and outbreak of a fiery mind,
A savageness in unreclaimed blood,
Of general assault.
    Rey.   But, my good lord—   35
    Pol.   Wherefore should you do this?
    Rey.   Ay, my lord,
I would know that.
    Pol.   Marry, sir, here 's my drift,
And I believe it is a fetch of warrant:
You laying these slight sullies on my son,
As 'twere a thing a little soil'd i' th' working,   40
Mark you,
Your party in converse, him you would sound,
Having ever seen in the prenominate crimes
The youth you breathe of guilty, be assur'd
He closes with you in this consequence—   45
"Good sir" or so, or "friend" or "gentleman"
According to the phrase or the addition
Of man and country.
    Rey.   Very good, my lord.
    Pol.   And then, sir, does 'a this—'a does—What was I
about to say? By the mass, I was about to say something;
where did I leave?
    Rey.   At "closes in the consequence", at "friend or so"
        and "gentleman".
    Pol.   At "closes in the consequence"—ay, marry,
He closes thus: "I know the gentleman;   55
I saw him yesterday, or t' other day,
Or then, or then; with such, or such; and, as you say,
There was 'a gaming; there o'ertook in 's rouse;
There falling out at tennis"; or perchance
"I saw him enter such a house of sale",   60
Videlicet, a brothel, or so forth. See you now
Your bait of falsehood take this carp of truth;
And thus do we of wisdom and of reach,

30. **open to incontinency:** either *liable to be accused of debauchery* or *addicted to debauchery*.

31. **breathe:** whisper. **quaintly:** artfully; ingeniously.

34. **unreclaimed:** untamed. The metaphor is from the sport of falconry, to *reclaim* being to recall a hawk from its flight.

35. **Of general assault:** to which we are all exposed.

38. **a fetch of warrant:** a device warranted, or certain, to succeed.

42. **him:** for *he*.

43-4. **Having ever . . . guilty:** if he has ever seen Laertes committing the crimes you are accusing him of. **prenominate:** aforesaid.

45. **He closes . . . in consequence:** he falls in with you to this effect.

47. **addition:** title.

58. **o'ertook in 's rouse:** overcome while drinking; drunk.

62. **carp:** a difficult fish to land. Polonius is also quibbling with the meaning *to reprehend*, implying that the truth will be derogatory.

63. **reach:** capacity.

With windlasses and with assays of bias,
By indirections find directions out;   65
So, by my former lecture and advice,
Shall you my son. You have me, have you not?
    Rey. My lord, I have.
    Pol.   God buy ye; fare ye well.
    Rey. Good my lord!
    Pol. Observe his inclination in yourself.   70
    Rey. I shall, my lord.
    Pol. And let him ply his music.
    Rey.   Well, my lord.
    Pol. Farewell!
                            [*Exit* REYNALDO.

               Enter OPHELIA.

How now, Ophelia! What 's the matter?
    Oph. O my lord, my lord, I have been so affrighted!   75
    Pol. With what, i' th' name of God?
    Oph. My lord, as I was sewing in my closet,
Lord Hamlet, with his doublet all unbrac'd,
No hat upon his head, his stockings fouled,
Ungart'red and down-gyved to his ankle;   80
Pale as his shirt, his knees knocking each other,
And with a look so piteous in purport
As if he had been loosed out of hell
To speak of horrors—he comes before me.
    Pol. Mad for thy love?
    Oph.   My lord, I do not know,   85
But truly I do fear it.
    Pol.   What said he?
    Oph. He took me by the wrist, and held me hard;
Then goes he to the length of all his arm,
And, with his other hand thus o'er his brow,
He falls to such perusal of my face   90
As 'a would draw it. Long stay'd he so.
At last, a little shaking of mine arm,
And thrice his head thus waving up and down,
He rais'd a sigh so piteous and profound
As it did seem to shatter all his bulk   95

64. **windlasses**: winding, circuitous paths. **assays of bias**: indirect attempts. The image is from bowls, in which the player uses the *bias*, the special shape, or weighting, of the bowl to send it in a curving path.

65. **indirections**: indirect ways.

66. **lecture**: instructions.

68. **God buy ye**: the usual Shakespearian form, indicating the pronunciation, of *God be with you.*

70. **in yourself**: for yourself. The line may mean, "Note his attitude towards you".

72. **let him ... music**: Let him go his own way. After what Polonius expects Laertes to be doing, it is hardly likely that this is an instruction for him to work at his music lessons!

77. **closet**: private room.

78. **doublet**: a close-fitting jacket worn in Elizabethan times, with or without sleeves and short skirts. **unbrac'd**: unfastened.

Some would say that Hamlet is pretending to be a desolate lover, and quote *As You Like It*, III. ii. 352-6: "Your hose should be ungarter'd, your bonnet unbanded, your sleeve unbutton'd, your shoe untied, and every thing about you demonstrating a careless desolation". All this, however, is carelessness to details, and not the complete disorder described by Ophelia.

80. **down-gyved**: *i.e.* having fallen down about his ankles like fetters or gyves.

90. **perusal**: intent study.

And end his being.   That done, he lets me go,
And, with his head over his shoulder turn'd,
He seem'd to find his way without his eyes;
For out adoors he went without their helps
And to the last bended their light on me.   100
    Pol.   Come, go with me.   I will go seek the King.
This is the very ecstasy of love,
Whose violent property fordoes itself,
And leads the will to desperate undertakings
As oft as any passion under heaven   105
That does afflict our natures.   I am sorry—
What, have you given him any hard words of late?
    Oph.   No, my good lord; but, as you did command,
I did repel his letters, and denied
His access to me.
    Pol.   That hath made him mad.   110
I am sorry that with better heed and judgment
I had not quoted him.   I fear'd he did but trifle,
And meant to wreck thee; but beshrew my jealousy!
By heaven, it is as proper to our age
To cast beyond ourselves in our opinions   115
As it is common for the younger sort
To lack discretion.   Come, go we to the King.
This must be known; which being kept close, might move
More grief to hide than hate to utter love.
Come.
                                                    [*Exeunt.*

SCENE II.   *Elsinore.   The Castle.*

Flourish.   Enter KING, QUEEN, ROSENCRANTZ,
GUILDENSTERN, *and* ATTENDANTS.

    King.   Welcome, dear Rosencrantz and Guildenstern!
Moreover that we much did long to see you,
The need we have to use you did provoke
Our hasty sending.   Something have you heard
Of Hamlet's transformation; so I call it,   5
Sith nor th' exterior nor the inward man
Resembles that it was.   What it should be,
More than his father's death, that thus hath put him

100. **bended their light**: fixed their gaze. In Shakespeare's time, light rays were vaguely thought of as emanating from the eyes. Thus we often find references to "eye-beames".

102. **ecstasy**: madness.

103. **property**: nature; character. **fordoes**: destroys.

106. **I am sorry**: Polonius breaks off, but completes the thought in line 111.

112. **quoted**: observed; noted.

113. **wreck**: ruin; seduce. **beshrew my jealousy**: curse my suspicion.

114-17. **it is as proper, . . . discretion**: it is as common for old men to be over-cunning as it is for the young to be rash. **proper**: natural. **To cast**: to plan; devise.

118-19. **which being kept . . . love**: It might cause more grief to hide the cause of Hamlet's madness, than anger to disclose his love for a commoner. Polonius need not have feared, however, for Gertrude had hoped for a union between the two (V. i. 234).

ACT II. SCENE II

2. **Moreover that**: in addition to the fact that.

6. **Sith**: since.

So much from th' understanding of himself,
I cannot deem of. I entreat you both   10
That, being of so young days brought up with him,
And sith so neighboured to his youth and haviour,
That you vouchsafe your rest here in our court
Some little time; so by your companies
To draw him on to pleasures, and to gather,   15
So much as from occasion you may glean,
Whether aught to us unknown afflicts him thus
That, open'd, lies within our remedy.
   Queen. Good gentlemen, he hath much talk'd of you;
And sure I am two men there is not living   20
To whom he more adheres. If it will please you
To show us so much gentry and good will
As to expend your time with us awhile
For the supply and profit of our hope,
Your visitation shall receive such thanks   25
As fits a king's remembrance.
   Ros.   Both your Majesties
Might, by the sovereign power you have of us,
Put your dread pleasures more into command
Than to entreaty.
   Guil.   But we both obey,
And here give up ourselves, in the full bent,   30
To lay our service freely at your feet,
To be commanded.
   King. Thanks, Rosencrantz and gentle Guildenstern.
   Queen. Thanks, Guildenstern and gentle Rosencrantz.
And I beseech you instantly to visit   35
My too much changed son. Go, some of you,
And bring these gentlemen where Hamlet is.
   Guil. Heavens make our presence and our practices
Pleasant and helpful to him!
   Queen.   Aye amen!   [*Exeunt*
     Rosencrantz, Guildenstern, *and some* Attendants.
             Enter Polonius.
   Pol. Th' ambassadors from Norway, my good lord, 40
Are joyfully return'd.

11. **of so young days:** from such early days; *i.e.* from boyhood.

12. **sith so neighboured . . . haviour:** afterwards so close to him in age and interests.

13. **vouchsafe your rest:** agree to stay.

16. **occasion:** favourable or suitable opportunity.

18. **open'd:** disclosed.

22. **gentry:** courtesy.

24. **supply and profit:** aid and benefit.

25. **visitation:** visit.

30. **in the full bent:** to the fullest extent. The metaphor is from archery, where *bent* is the straining of the bow.

38. **practices:** doings; actions. This may be dramatic irony, in that although Guildenstern intends the word in a good sense, the audience can give it the bad one of *intrigues*.

King. Thou still hast been the father of good news.

Pol. Have I, my lord? I assure you, my good liege,
I hold my duty, as I hold my soul,
Both to my God and to my gracious King;   45
And I do think—or else this brain of mine
Hunts not the trail of policy so sure
As it hath us'd to do—that I have found
The very cause of Hamlet's lunacy.

King. O speak of that; that do I long to hear.   50

Pol. Give first admittance to th' ambassadors;
My news shall be the fruit to that great feast.

King. Thyself do grace to them, and bring them in.

                                [Exit POLONIUS.

He tells me, my dear Gertrude, he hath found
The head and source of all your son's distemper.   55

Queen. I doubt it is no other but the main,
His father's death and our o'erhasty marriage.

King. Well, we shall sift him.

    Re-enter POLONIUS, *with* VOLTEMAND *and* CORNELIUS.

                        Welcome, my good friends!
Say, Voltemand, what from our brother Norway?

Volt. Most fair return of greetings and desires.   60
Upon our first, he sent out to suppress
His nephew's levies; which to him appear'd
To be a preparation 'gainst the Polack;
But, better look'd into, he truly found
It was against your Highness. Whereat griev'd,   65
That so his sickness, age, and impotence,
Was falsely borne in hand, sends out arrests
On Fortinbras; which he, in brief, obeys;
Receives rebuke from Norway; and, in fine,
Makes vow before his uncle never more   70
To give th' assay of arms against your Majesty.
Whereon old Norway, overcome with joy,
Gives him threescore thousand crowns in annual fee,
And his commission to employ those soldiers,
So levied as before, against the Polack;   75

42. **still**: always; ever.

48. **it hath us'd**: it used to do.
49. **very**: true.

52. **fruit**: *i.e.* dessert, the last course.

56. **the main**: the chief cause.

61. **Upon our first**: on our first request; at once.

67. **borne in hand**: abused; deluded. **arrests**: *i.e.* orders to stop him

69. **in fine**: in the end; finally.

71. **assay**: trial; proof.

With an entreaty, herein further shown,   [*Gives a paper.*
That it might please you to give quiet pass
Through your dominions for this enterprise,
On such regards of safety and allowance
As therein are set down.

   King.   It likes us well;   80
And at our more considered time we 'll read,
Answer, and think upon this business.
Meantime we thank you for your well-took labour.
Go to your rest; at night we 'll feast together.
Most welcome home!

                   [*Exeunt* AMBASSADORS *and* ATTENDANTS.
   Pol.   This business is well ended.   85
My liege, and madam, to expostulate
What majesty should be, what duty is,
Why day is day, night night, and time is time,
Were nothing, but to waste night, day, and time.
Therefore, since brevity is the soul of wit,   90
And tediousness the limbs and outward flourishes,
I will be brief.   Your noble son is mad.
Mad call I it; for, to define true madness,
What is 't but to be nothing else but mad?
But let that go.

   Queen.   More matter with less art.   95
   Pol.   Madam, I swear I use no art at all.
That he 's mad 'tis true: 'tis true 'tis pity;
And pity 'tis 'tis true.   A foolish figure!
But farewell it, for I will use no art.
Mad let us grant him, then; and now remains   100
That we find out the cause of this effect;
Or rather say the cause of this defect,
For this effect defective comes by cause.
Thus it remains, and the remainder thus.
Perpend.   105
I have a daughter—have while she is mine—
Who in her duty and obedience, mark,
Hath given me this.   Now gather, and surmise.   [*Reads.*
   "To the celestial, and my soul's idol, the most beautified

79. **regards of safety and allowance:** conditions for the safety of
Denmark and for the permission to be granted.

81. **more considered time:** a time more fitted for reflection.

86. **expostulate:** discourse on.

90. **wit:** wisdom.

96. **art:** Polonius is embellishing his speech excessively with the
rhetorical devices taught in Elizabethan schools.
98. **figure:** a device of rhetoric; a figure of speech.

103. **this effect . . . cause:** this effect, which is a defect, results from a
cause.
105. **Perpend:** consider. The word, like Polonius, is bombastic.

108. **gather, and surmise:** listen and then draw your conclusions.
109. **beautified:** the word seems to have been fairly common in
Shakespeare's time, and probably has no hint of "artificially made
beautiful". Polonius finds it unrefined.

Ophelia." That 's an ill phrase, a vile phrase; "beautified"
is a vile phrase. But you shall hear. Thus: [*Reads.*
   "In her excellent white bosom, these, &c".
   Queen. Came this from Hamlet to her?
   Pol. Good madam, stay awhile; I will be faithful.

                                               [*Reads.*

              "Doubt thou the stars are fire;   115
                 Doubt that the sun doth move;
              Doubt truth to be a liar;
                 But never doubt I love.

   O dear Ophelia, I am ill at these numbers.
I have not art to reckon my groans; but that I love thee best,
O most best, believe it. Adieu.

                         Thine evermore, most dear lady, whilst
                            this machine is to him, HAMLET."

This, in obedience, hath my daughter shown me;
And more above, hath his solicitings,   125
As they fell out by time, by means, and place,
All given to mine ear.
   King.   But how hath she
Receiv'd his love?
   Pol.   What do you think of me?
   King. As of a man faithful and honourable.
   Pol. I would fain prove so. But what might you think,
When I had seen this hot love on the wing,   131
As I perceiv'd it, I must tell you that,
Before my daughter told me—what might you,
Or my dear Majesty your queen here, think,
If I had play'd the desk or table-book;   135
Or given my heart a winking, mute and dumb;
Or look'd upon this love with idle sight—
What might you think? No, I went round to work,
And my young mistress thus I did bespeak:
"Lord Hamlet is a prince out of thy star;   140
This must not be". And then I prescripts gave her,
That she should lock herself from his resort,
Admit no messengers, receive no tokens.

112. **In her . . . bosom:** The allusion may be to the fact that in Shakespeare's time ladies had a pocket in the bosom of the dress. **these:** a common ending to the heading of a letter.

116. **Doubt . . . move:** The sun was then thought to move round the earth.
117. **Doubt:** suspect.

119. **ill at these numbers:** bad at writing verse.

123. **machine:** *i.e.* his body.   Hamlet belongs to Ophelia while he lives.

125. **more above:** moreover.

135-7. **play'd the desk . . . sight:** "If I had served as silent, but active intermediary between them, like a desk that acts as a receptacle for letters; or a memorandum book in which the lovers might write; or mutely and dumbly connived at the affair; or treated the affair as of no importance." **idle:** careless; negligent.
138. **round:** straightforwardly.
140. **out of thy star:** above you in fortune.   The modern expression, "out of your sphere", preserves the astrological allusion; see note on I. v. 17.
141. **prescripts:** commands.

Which done, she took the fruits of my advice;
And he repelled, a short tale to make,   145
Fell into a sadness, then into a fast,
Thence to a watch, thence into a weakness,
Thence to a lightness, and, by this declension,
Into the madness wherein now he raves
And all we mourn for.

King.   Do you think 'tis this?   150
Queen. It may be, very like.
Pol. Hath there been such a time—I would fain know
    that—
That I have positively said " 'Tis so",
When it prov'd otherwise?

King.   Not that I know.
Pol. Take this from this, if this be otherwise.   155
If circumstances lead me, I will find
Where truth is hid, though it were hid indeed
Within the centre.

King.   How may we try it further?
Pol. You know sometimes he walks four hours together,
Here in the lobby.

Queen.   So he does, indeed.   160
Pol. At such a time I 'll loose my daughter to him.
Be you and I behind an arras then;
Mark the encounter: if he love her not,
And be not from his reason fall'n thereon,
Let me be no assistant for a state,   165
But keep a farm and carters.

King.   We will try it.

Enter HAMLET, reading a book.

Queen. But look where sadly the poor wretch comes
    reading.
Pol. Away, I do beseech you, both away:
I 'll board him presently. O, give me leave.

[Exeunt KING and QUEEN.
How does my good Lord Hamlet?   170
Ham. Well, God-a-mercy.

144. **took the fruits of:** benefit by.

147. **watch:** wakefulness; sleeplessness.
148. **lightness:** light-headedness. **declension:** process of decline.

155. **Take this from this:** Usually interpreted as "Take my head from my shoulders", but it could equally probably refer to taking Polonius's chain of office from his neck, or his official staff from his hand.

158. **the centre:** *i.e.* of the earth.

161. **loose:** release. The word is used of animals at stud, and suggests "farm and carters" in line 166.
162. **arras:** tapestry, which would be hung on frames away from the wall, to avoid damage from damp.
164. **thereon:** for that cause.

167. **But look:** Dover Wilson, in *What Happens in "Hamlet"*, argues that Hamlet's actual entry, unknown to the others, is early enough to allow him to hear of the plot. This would account for the accusations and insinuations about Ophelia in the dialogue which follows, and give it more point. On the other hand, it would make the whole of the dialogue between Hamlet and Ophelia in the nunnery scene (III. i) into a bitter sparring match on Hamlet's side, instead of its having the strong dramatic effect of tenderness turning to anger as the Prince begins to suspect. **wretch:** a term expressing endearment and pity.
169. **board:** accost. **presently:** immediately.

Pol.   Do you know me, my lord?

Ham.   Excellent well; you are a fishmonger.

Pol.   Not I, my lord.

Ham.   Then I would you were so honest a man.   175

Pol.   Honest, my lord!

Ham.   Ay, sir; to be honest, as this world goes, is to be one man pick'd out of ten thousand.

Pol.   That 's very true, my lord.

Ham.   For if the sun breed maggots in a dead dog, being a good kissing carrion—Have you a daughter?   181

Pol.   I have, my lord.

Ham.   Let her not walk i' th' sun.   Conception is a blessing.   But as your daughter may conceive—friend, look to 't   185

Pol.   How say you by that? [*Aside.*] Still harping on my daughter.   Yet he knew me not at first; 'a said I was a fishmonger.   'A is far gone, far gone.   And truly in my youth I suff'red much extremity for love.   Very near this.   I 'll speak to him again.—What do you read, my lord?   190

Ham.   Words, words, words.

Pol.   What is the matter, my lord?

Ham.   Between who?

Pol.   I mean, the matter that you read, my lord.   194

Ham.   Slanders, sir; for the satirical rogue says here that old men have grey beards; that their faces are wrinkled; their eyes purging thick amber and plum-tree gum; and that they have a plentiful lack of wit, together with most weak hams—all which, sir, though I most powerfully and potently believe, yet I hold it not honesty to have it thus set down; for you yourself, sir, shall grow old as I am, if, like a crab, you could go backward.

Pol.   [*Aside.*]   Though this be madness, yet there is method in 't.—Will you walk out of the air, my lord?

Ham.   Into my grave?   205

Pol.   Indeed, that 's out of the air.   [*Aside.*]   How pregnant sometimes his replies are! a happiness that often madness hits on, which reason and sanity could not so

172. **Do you know me:** For all the diplomatic tact offered in his advice to Reynaldo, this abrupt approach is the best Polonius can do when accosting a man he believes to be mad!

173. **fishmonger:** Polonius is fishing for secrets, but the word was also a slang word for *bawd*, and *fishmonger's daughter* meant *prostitute*.

180. **if the sun breed maggots:** This was considered to be literally true, just as, "Your serpent of Egypt is bred now of your mud by the operation of your sun" (*Antony and Cleopatra*, II. vii. 26-7).

181. **good kissing carrion:** carrion good for kissing. The action of the sun is elsewhere referred to as "kissing", e.g. *I Henry IV*, II. iv. 114, "Did'st thou never see Titan kiss a dish of butter?" Carrion was used for "flesh" considered sexually, so that Hamlet is clearly harping on the subject of sexual relations with *fishmonger, breed, kissing, carrion*.

183. **walk i' th' sun:** Another punning reference to the proverb meaning "out of favour (with fortune)" (see note to I. ii. 67). Hamlet has possibly realised that Polonius has warned Ophelia against him, and is ironically echoing the warning, by referring to the sun's ability to breed in what it may shine on. Alternatively, if we accept Dover Wilson about the entry of Hamlet—see the note on line 167—then Hamlet is reacting to the use of the word *loose* in line 161.

186. **by that:** about that.

192. **matter:** *i.e.* subject matter. Hamlet takes it to mean *quarrel*, or perhaps, bearing in mind his other remarks, an *illicit love affair*.

195. **the satirical rogue:** Various writers have been suggested here, but surely we are to take it that Hamlet makes up all of the description from Polonius's own appearance.

197. **purging:** discharging. **amber:** resin.

200. **hold it not honesty:** consider it immoral.

201. **shall grow as old as I:** The phrasing makes it appear that Hamlet is indignant at the satire because it refers to himself, and that Polonius ought to be too, for he will also reach Hamlet's age eventually. The last phrase, however, makes it quite clear that Hamlet is aware of the true position, and that he is deliberately making fun of the old man.

204. **out of the air:** Polonius wishes Hamlet to come out of the fresh air, considered harmful to a sick man. Hamlet takes him absolutely literally.

206. **pregnant:** meaningful.

207. **happiness:** *i.e.* of phrase or expression.

prosperously be delivered of. I will leave him, and suddenly contrive the means of meeting between him and my
daughter.—My lord. I will take my leave of you.   211

Ham. You cannot, sir, take from me anything that I will
more willingly part withal—except my life, except my life,
except my life.

Enter ROSENCRANTZ *and* GUILDENSTERN.

Pol. Fare you well, my lord.   215
Ham. These tedious old fools!
Pol. You go to seek the Lord Hamlet; there he is.
Ros. [*To* POLONIUS.] God save you, sir!

[*Exit* POLONIUS.

Guil. My honour'd lord!
Ros. My most dear lord!   220
Ham. My excellent good friends! How dost thou,
Guildenstern? Ah, Rosencrantz! Good lads, how do you
both?

Ros. As the indifferent children of the earth.
Guil. Happy in that we are not over-happy;   225
On fortune's cap we are not the very button.
Ham. Nor the soles of her shoe?
Ros. Neither, my lord.
Ham. Then you live about her waist, or in the middle of
her favours?   230
Guil. Faith, her privates we.
Ham. In the secret parts of Fortune? O, most true; she
is a strumpet. What news?
Ros. None, my lord, but that the world 's grown honest.
Ham. Then is doomsday near. But your news is not true.
Let me question more in particular. What have you, my
good friends, deserved at the hands of Fortune, that she
sends you to prison hither?
Guil. Prison, my lord!
Ham. Denmark 's a prison.   240
Ros. Then is the world one.
Ham. A goodly one; in which there are many confines,
wards, and dungeons, Denmark being one o' th' worst.

214. **except my life**: Coleridge remarks, "This repetition strikes me as most admirable". Bradley considers it a mark of Hamlet's character, and certainly Hamlet does tend to repeat phrases.

221. **My excellent good friends**: Hamlet receives his friends cordially, but soon detects that they are sent to spy on him.

224. **indifferent**: ordinary; average.

238. **to prison**: Rosencrantz and Guildenstern have obviously come from abroad, possibly from Wittenberg.

242. **confines**: places of confinement.

Ros. We think not so, my lord.   244

Ham. Why, then, 'tis none to you; for there is nothing either good or bad, but thinking makes it so. To me it is a prison.

Ros. Why, then your ambition makes it one; 'tis too narrow for your mind.   249

Ham. O God, I could be bounded in a nutshell and count myself a king of infinite space, were it not that I have bad dreams.

Guil. Which dreams indeed are ambition; for the very substance of the ambitious is merely the shadow of a dream.

Ham. A dream itself is but a shadow.   255

Ros. Truly, and I hold ambition of so airy and light a quality that it is but a shadow's shadow.

Ham. Then are our beggars bodies, and our monarchs and outstretch'd heroes the beggars' shadows. Shall we to th' court? for, by my fay, I cannot reason.   260

Both. We 'll wait upon you.

Ham. No such matter. I will not sort you with the rest of my servants; for, to speak to you like an honest man, I am most dreadfully attended. But, in the beaten way of friendship, what make you at Elsinore?   265

Ros. To visit you, my lord; no other occasion.

Ham. Beggar that I am, I am even poor in thanks; but I thank you; and sure, dear friends, my thanks are too dear a half-penny. Were you not sent for? Is it your own inclining? Is it a free visitation? Come, come, deal justly with me. Come, come; nay, speak.   271

Guil. What should we say, my lord?

Ham. Why any thing. But to th' purpose; you were sent for; and there is a kind of confession in your looks, which your modesties have not craft enough to colour; I know the good King and Queen have sent for you.   276

Ros. To what end, my lord?

Ham. That you must teach me. But let me conjure you by the rights of our fellowship, by the consonancy of our youth, by the obligation of our ever-preserved love, and by

245-6. there is nothing . . . so: Whether a thing is good or bad depends on how the mind regards it.

248. ambition: Rosencrantz is trying "by indirection" to discover whether Hamlet is disappointed at not having succeeded his father.

253-4. the very substance . . . dream: *i.e.* that of which the ambitious man is made (*i.e.* what he has achieved of his desires) is so unlike what he dreamt of attaining that it is only the shadow of his dream. Thus the ambitious man is a mere shadow.

258-9. Then are our beggars . . . shadows: The reasoning by which this conclusion is reached goes as follows: The ambitious are, according to Guildenstern (line 254) made up of shadows, so that the *only* solid bodies are those unambitious enough to be beggars. Kings and great heroes, on the other hand, being the most successfully ambitious of men, are shadows, which, since shadows must be cast by solid bodies, are the shadows of the beggars. **outstretch'd:** puffed up; pretentious.

260. fay: faith. Hamlet, tired of this intellectual quibbling, ends it with a paradox to expose its ridiculousness, and suggests that they should go to the Court, where reason is not required.

261. wait upon: *attend,* but there is also possibly a hint taken by Hamlet, of *lie in wait for.*

262. sort you: class you; associate you.

264. dreadfully attended: alluding to his servants. Is Hamlet hinting at his lowly position? Although he says and does little directly to confirm the King's suspicions that he wants the throne, he refers often to his poverty, *e.g.* line 267. Even if he was unambitious, Hamlet must have found it galling to see the murderer, Claudius, enjoy a position which might have been his own. This is not to suggest that it has any special bearing on Hamlet's state of mind, only that he must naturally have such feelings.

268-9. dear a half-penny: not worth a half-penny. Hamlet, suspicious after their attempts to discover his "ambitions", and the clue of line 261, may *really* be saying that a half-penny-worth of thanks is too much to pay.

270. inclining: inclination; desire (*i.e.* which has brought you here).

273. to th' purpose: to the point.

275. modesties: sense of shame. **colour:** disguise.

279. consonancy: harmony; accord.

what more dear a better proposer can charge you withal, be
even and direct with me, whether you were sent for or no?

Ros. [*Aside to* GUILDENSTERN.] What say you?

Ham. [*Aside.*] Nay, then, I have an eye of you.—If you
love me, hold not off.   285

Guil. My lord, we were sent for.

Ham. I will tell you why; so shall my anticipation prevent your discovery, and your secrecy to the King and Queen
moult no feather. I have of late—but wherefore I know not
—lost all my mirth, forgone all custom of exercises; and
indeed it goes so heavily with my disposition that this goodly
frame, the earth, seems to me a sterile promontory; this most
excellent canopy the air, look you, this brave o'er-hanging
firmament, this majestical roof fretted with golden fire—why,
it appeareth no other thing to me than a foul and pestilent
congregation of vapours. What a piece of work is a man!
How noble in reason! how infinite in faculties! in form and
moving, how express and admirable! in action, how like
an angel! in apprehension, how like a god! the beauty of
the world! the paragon of animals! And yet, to me, what
is this quintessence of dust? Man delights not me—no, nor
woman neither, though by your smiling you seem to say so.

Ros. My lord, there was no such stuff in my thoughts.

Ham. Why did ye laugh, then, when I said "Man delights
not me"?   305

Ros. To think, my lord, if you delight not in man, what
lenten entertainment the players shall receive from you. We
coted them on the way; and hither are they coming to offer
you service.   309

Ham. He that plays the king shall be welcome—his
Majesty shall have tribute on me; the adventurous knight
shall use his foil and target; the lover shall not sigh gratis;
the humorous man shall end his part in peace; the clown
shall make those laugh whose lungs are tickle a' th' sere; and
the lady shall say her mind freely, or the blank verse shall
halt for 't. What players are they?   316

Ros. Even those you were wont to take such delight in—
the tragedians of the city.

281. **a better proposer:** a more skilful advocate.
282. **even:** just; fair; honest.

284. **of:** on.

287-9. **prevent your discovery . . . feather:** anticipate your having to disclose the facts, so that your promise of secrecy to the King and Queen shall not be broken.

292. **frame:** structure.
293. **brave:** fine. The sense survives in the expression "a brave sight."
294. **fretted:** adorned; decorated (with stars).

297. **faculties:** abilities.
298. **express:** active; purposeful, *or* well-framed; modelled.

307. **lenten entertainment:** meagre welcome.
308. **coted:** caught up with and passed. It was a term in hunting.
311. **on:** of; from.
312. **foil and target:** sword and round shield. **gratis:** for nothing; in vain—*i.e.* Hamlet will applaud.
313. **humorous man:** not the clown, mentioned next, but the man full of "humours" (see note to I. iv. 27-8), often represented as capricious or quarrelsome. **in peace** is therefore a pun on the meanings *without interruption*, and *peacefully*.
314. **tickle a' th' sere:** easily moved to laughter. The image is of a gun with a **sere** (which holds back the hammer) tripped by the slightest pressure.
315-16. **the lady . . . halt for 't:** Again two meanings: (1) The lady will be allowed to say her lines without interruption, (2) The lady will say her lines without omitting any indecent parts, otherwise the irregular limping metre of the verse will betray the fact. The lady, of course, would be a boy actor; female performers were virtually unknown in England until after the Restoration. **halt:** limp.
318. **the city:** We may be intended to understand Wittenberg here, but the references which follow are all to the London of Shakespeare's day.

Ham. How chances it they travel? Their residence, both
in reputation and profit, was better both ways.   320

Ros. I think their inhibition comes by the means of the
late innovation.

Ham. Do they hold the same estimation they did when I
was in the city? Are they so followed?

Ros. No, indeed, are they not.   325

Ham. How comes it? Do they grow rusty?

Ros. Nay, their endeavour keeps in the wonted pace; but
there is, sir, an eyrie of children, little eyases, that cry out
on the top of question, and are most tyrannically clapp'd for
't. These are now the fashion, and so berattle the common
stages—so they call them—that many wearing rapiers are
afraid of goose quills and dare scarce come thither.   332

Ham. What, are they children? Who maintains 'em?
How are they escoted? Will they pursue the quality no
longer than they can sing? Will they not say afterwards, if
they should grow themselves to common players—as it is
most like, if their means are no better—their writers do them
wrong to make them exclaim against their own succession?

Ros. Faith, there has been much to-do on both sides; and
the nation holds it no sin to tarre them to controversy. There
was for a while no money bid for argument, unless the poet
and the player went to cuffs in the question.   342

Ham. Is 't possible?

Guil. O, there has been much throwing about of brains.

Ham. Do the boys carry it away?   345

Ros. Ay, that they do, my lord—Hercules and his load
too.

Ham. It is not very strange; for my uncle is King of
Denmark, and those that would make mows at him while
my father lived give twenty, forty, fifty, a hundred ducats
apiece for his picture in little. 'S blood, there is something
in this more than natural, if philosophy could find it out. 352
                                              [*A flourish.*

Guil. There are the players.   353

Ham. Gentlemen, you are welcome to Elsinore. Your
hands, come then; th' appurtenance of welcome is fashion

319. **they travel:** There are good grounds for thinking that Shakespeare's company, the Lord Chamberlain's Servants, travelled in 1601: they appear to have been at Aberdeen and Cambridge. The name of *tragedians* (line 318), however, is felt by some to be more fittingly applied to the Lord Admiral's Men, with its famous actor Edward Alleyn, who performed in Marlowe's tragedies; Shakespeare's company was noted more for comedy. Moreover, it is unlikely that Shakespeare would write of his *own* company's waning reputation, in line 325.

321. **inhibition:** technically an official prohibition to perform plays, but here used merely to denote a voluntary stoppage.

322. **the late innovation:** Probably the boy actors of the lines 328-32. We find, however, that *innovation* was very often used of a political upheaval, and Dover Wilson would have it that there is reference to an official prohibition after the rising by the Earl of Essex in 1601.

328. **eyrie:** nest of a bird of prey, here used in the sense of *a nest-ful, a brood.* **eyases:** unfledged hawks. These boy actors performed at the Blackfriars Theatre from 1600 on, and were very popular. See Introduction, p. 7.

329. **on the top of question:** so loudly that they sound out above all others in the controversy. **tyrannically:** violently; extravagantly; referring to the noisy manner of performing the part of a tyrant on the stage (*cf.* note to III. ii. 12).

330. **berattle:** fill or assail with din. **common stages:** ordinary, public theatres.

331-2. **many wearing . . . thither:** Many gallants (wearing rapiers) are afraid of the satirical pens of the writers for the children's theatre, and scarcely dare to attend an ordinary theatre.

334. **escoted:** paid; maintained. **pursue the quality:** follow the profession (used very frequently of acting).

338. **exclaim against their own succession:** cry out against their own future.

340. **tarre:** incite; set on.

341-2. **no money bid . . . question:** the public would not pay to see a play, however good the plot, unless it contained speeches carrying on the controversy. **argument:** plot; subject matter.

345. **carry it away:** win the day

346-7. **Hercules and his load too:** Referring to the Globe Theatre, whose sign was Hercules carrying the world. **too** seems to imply "as well as the tragedians of the city" of whom they have been speaking. (See note to line 319.)

348. **It is not very strange:** The boys' popularity is no stranger than that of Hamlet's uncle.

349. **mows:** grimaces.

351. **picture in little:** a miniature.

355. **appurtenance:** proper accompaniment.

and ceremony.   Let me comply with you in this garb; lest
my extent to the players, which, I tell you, must show fairly
outwards, should more appear like entertainment than yours.
You are welcome.   But my uncle-father and aunt-mother are
deceived.   360
    Guil.   In what, my dear lord?
    Ham.   I am but mad north-north-west; when the wind is
southerly I know a hawk from a handsaw.

Re-enter POLONIUS.

    Pol.   Well be with you, gentlemen!   364
    Ham.   Hark you, Guildenstern, and you too—at each ear
a hearer: that great baby you see there is not yet out of his
swaddling clouts.
    Ros.   Happily he is the second time come to them; for
they say an old man is twice a child.   369
    Ham.   I will prophesy he comes to tell me of the players;
mark it.   You say right, sir: a Monday morning; 'twas then
indeed.
    Pol.   My lord, I have news to tell you.
    Ham.   My lord, I have news to tell you.
When Roscius was an actor in Rome—   375
    Pol.   The actors are come hither, my lord.
    Ham.   Buzz, buzz!
    Pol.   Upon my honour—
    Ham.   Then came each actor on his ass—   379
    Pol.   The best actors in the world, either for tragedy,
comedy, history, pastoral, pastoral-comical, historical-pas-
toral, tragical-historical, tragical-comical-historical-pastoral,
scene individable, or poem unlimited.   Seneca cannot be too
heavy nor Plautus too light.   For the law of writ and the
liberty, these are the only men.   385
    Ham.   O Jephthah, judge of Israel, what a treasure hadst
thou!
    Pol.   What a treasure had he, my lord?
    Ham.   Why—

"One fair daughter, and no more,   390
The which he loved passing well".

356. **comply with . . . garb:** observe the ceremonies in this fashion. Though the speech appears to be friendly (meaning that close friends need not shake hands, but Hamlet ought to in order to demonstrate to others that his friends are at least as welcome as the players) the implication may be that they had better try to keep up the appearance of friendship.

357. **extent:** show of courtesy. **show fairly outwards:** make a good outward impression.

358. **entertainment:** favourable reception.

362. **mad north-north-west:** only occasionally or a trifle mad. There was a belief that the prevailing winds affected people suffering from mental diseases.

363. **a hawk from a handsaw:** The most feasible explanation of this is that *handsaw* is a corruption of *heronshaw*, a species of heron (still pronounced *harnsa* in East Anglia). Thus, Hamlet says that when the two birds fly with the south wind, *away* from the sun, he can distinguish a bird of prey from something harmless, implying that given the chances he has had, he can recognise his enemies. This, however, might be a quibble, hidden under the possible basic meaning of two tools, for **hawk** is still used of a plasterer's mortar board, while in Elizabethan times *a hack* was a kind of pick-axe.

368. **Happily:** haply; perhaps.

375. **Roscius:** A celebrated Roman actor.

377. **Buzz, buzz:** stale news!

379. **Then came . . . ass:** Probably a line from a ballad. Hamlet uses it to make the rude pun on "upon mine honour".

383. **scene individable:** a play which observed the unities of time, place, and action, in contrast with a **poem unlimited**, which did not. **Seneca:** A Roman philosopher, who also wrote tragedies which had great influence on Elizabethan dramatists. His plays were notable for their use of the supernatural, their retailing of violence and horrors, and their rhetorical, ranting language. *Hamlet* itself is an example of how Seneca influenced Elizabethan taste.

384. **Plautus:** The first and greatest of the Roman comic dramatists. **the law of writ and the liberty:** plays which follow the rules (*e.g.* follow the unities) and those which disregard them. Some editors explain "for repeating faithfully what is in the text, or extemporising".

386. **Jephthah:** To keep an oath sworn to God, Jephthah sacrificed his only daughter. Hamlet is alluding to an old ballad, one version of which can be found in Percy's *Reliques*, Book II. Dover Wilson suggests that the reason Hamlet first alludes to Jephthah is that Polonius's speech is a "satirical epitome of the repertory and perhaps even the play-bills of the Admiral's men", who, it seems, performed a play called *Jephthah* in 1601.

Pol. [*Aside.*] Still on my daughter.

Ham. Am I not i' th' right, old Jephthah?

Pol. If you call me Jephthah, my lord, I have a daughter
that I love passing well.   395

Ham. Nay, that follows not.

Pol. What follows then, my lord?

Ham. Why—

        "As by lot, God wot"

and then, you know,   400

        "It came to pass, as most like it was".

The first row of the pious chanson will show you more;
for look where my abridgement comes.

Enter the PLAYERS.

You are welcome, masters; welcome, all.—I am glad to see
thee well. Welcome, good friends.—O, my old friend! Why
thy face is valanc'd since I saw thee last; com'st thou to
beard me in Denmark?—What, my young lady and
mistress! By 'r lady, your ladyship is nearer to heaven
than when I saw you last by the altitude of a chopine.
Pray God, your voice, like a piece of uncurrent gold,
be not crack'd within the ring.—Masters, you are all
welcome. We 'll e'en to 't like French falconers, fly at
anything we see. We 'll have a speech straight. Come,
give us a taste of your quality; come, a passionate
speech.   415

First Play. What speech, my good lord?

Ham. I heard thee speak me a speech once, but it was
never acted; or, if it was, not above once; for the play, I
remember, pleas'd not the million; 'twas caviary to the
general. But it was—as I received it, and others whose
judgments in such matters cried in the top of mine—an
excellent play, well digested in the scenes, set down with as
much modesty as cunning. I remember one said there were
no sallets in the lines to make the matter savoury, nor no
matter in the phrase that might indict the author of affectation; but call'd it an honest method, as wholesome as sweet,
and by very much more handsome than fine. One speech in
it I chiefly lov'd: 'twas Æneas' tale to Dido; and thereabout

392. my daughter: Polonius assumes that Hamlet, mad for love, makes the reference because he, Polonius, is Ophelia's father. He could be right, and also, if we believe Dover Wilson's theory that Hamlet knows of Polonius's plot to "loose his daughter" to him (see note to line 167), the reference could be to the "sacrifice" of Ophelia to this plot. **Still:** always.

396. that follows not: It does not follow that because I call you Jephthah, you must therefore have a daughter.

399. As by lot: Hamlet now takes *follows* to mean *comes next* (in the ballad).

402. row: stanza. **chanson:** song; ballad.

403. abridgement: "that which cuts short my remarks", or possibly, "entertainment" as it is used in M.S.N.D., V. i. 39, "Say what abridgement have you for this evening?"

406. valanc'd: fringed with a beard.

407. my young lady: Hamlet is addressing a boy actor who took female roles.

409. chopine: A kind of high shoe, worn especially in Venice. According to Coryat in his *Crudities* (1611), some were half a yard high.

411. crack'd within the ring: Coins of the period had a ring encircling the sovereign's head. If it was cracked or worn within this ring, it was unfit for currency.

412. French falconers: Dover Wilson shows that the French were "master-falconers of the age", so that their readiness to "fly at anything" demonstrated their skill, and is not a sneer.

414. quality: art. The word is used in the same sense as in line 334.

417. speak me: This idiom does not imply that the speech was spoken for Hamlet in particular.

419-20. caviary to the general: *i.e.* above the heads of the common people. Caviare was first introduced into England in Elizabeth's reign, and was then, as now, considered a great delicacy. Shakespeare's allusion is based on the fact that it generally proves unpalatable when first tried.

421. cried in the top of mine: excelled mine. The metaphor is from a pack of hounds, the better dogs baying more loudly on the scent.

422. digested: arranged.

423. modesty: moderation; restraint. **cunning:** skill.

424. sallets: salads of spicy herbs. Hamlet means improper remarks. We preserve the same sort of sense in "spicy story".

427. more handsome than fine: more dignified than splendidly ornamented.

428. Æneas' tale to Dido: It is probable that Shakespeare had in his mind *Dido, Queen of Carthage*, a play by Marlowe and Nash, though he is not copying any particular speech. Most of the echoes discovered are from Virgil's *Æneid*. He may have been writing burlesque, as some critics believe, but if so, we must believe that Hamlet's remarks about the speech were ironical, since we are surely meant to take his remarks on actors and acting (III. ii) as those of an intelligent critic. Most probably, the speech was written in this earlier style to mark it out as a play within a play. After all, how else *could* Shakespeare have distinguished it?

of it especially where he speaks of Priam's slaughter. If it
live in your memory, begin at this line—let me see, let me
see :   431
   "The rugged Pyrrhus, like th' Hyrcanian beast,"
'Tis not so; it begins with Pyrrhus.
"The rugged Pyrrhus, he whose sable arms,
Black as his purpose, did the night resemble   435
When he lay couched in the ominous horse,
Hath now this dread and black complexion smear'd
With heraldry more dismal; head to foot
Now is he total gules, horridly trick'd
With blood of fathers, mothers, daughters, sons,   440
Bak'd and impasted with the parching streets,
That lend a tyrannous and damned light
To their lord's murder. Roasted in wrath and fire,
And thus o'er-sized with coagulate gore,
With eyes like carbuncles, the hellish Pyrrhus   445
Old grandsire Priam seeks."
So proceed you.
  Pol. Fore God, my lord, well spoken, with good accent
and good discretion.
  First Play.   "Anon he finds him   450
Striking too short at Greeks; his antique sword,
Rebellious to his arm, lies where it falls,
Repugnant to command. Unequal match'd,
Pyrrhus at Priam drives, in rage strikes wide;
But with the whiff and wind of his fell sword   455
Th' unnerved father falls. Then senseless Ilium,
Seeming to feel this blow, with flaming top
Stoops to his base, and with a hideous crash
Takes prisoner Pyrrhus' ear. For, lo! his sword,
Which was declining on the milky head   460
Of reverend Priam, seem'd i' th' air to stick.
So, as a painted tyrant, Pyrrhus stood
And, like a neutral to his will and matter,
Did nothing.
But as we often see, against some storm,   465
A silence in the heavens, the rack stand still,

432. **Hyrcanian beast:** Hyrcania was an area on the south and south-east of the Caspian Sea, famous in ancient times for wild beasts, especially *tigers*.

436. **couched:** like a wild beast ready to spring.   **ominous horse:** the wooden horse with which the Greeks took Troy.

439. **gules:** an heraldic term meaning *red*.   **trick'd:** a description in drawing in heraldry, as opposed to *blazon* which is a description in words.
441-3. **Bak'd ... murder:** the blazing buildings heat the blood on Pyrrhus until it clots, and illuminate the murder of Priam.

444. **o'er-sized:** covered with size, a kind of weak glue.   **coagulate:** clotted.
445. **carbuncles:** red precious stones, said to emit light like glowing coal.

453. **Repugnant to:** resisting.

455. **with the whiff ... sword:** This echoes *Dido, Queen of Carthage:*

"Which he, disdaining, whisked his sword about,
    And with the wind thereof the King fell down."

456. **senseless:** without feelings.   **Ilium:** Troy.
458. **his:** its.
459-61. **Takes prisoner ... stick:** The crash alarms and stupefies Pyrrhus so much that for a moment he stands incapable of action.

462. **a painted tyrant:** "like a tyrant in a painting", but also, of course, "painted with blood".
463. **neutral to his will and matter:** like someone indifferent to his desire and the business he had to do.
465. **against:** before.
466. **rack:** the mass of clouds.

The bold wind speechless, and the orb below
As hush as death, anon the dreadful thunder
Doth rend the region; so, after Pyrrhus' pause,
A roused vengeance sets him new a-work;   470
And never did the Cyclops' hammers fall
On Mars's armour, forg'd for proof eterne,
With less remorse than Pyrrhus' bleeding sword
Now falls on Priam.

Out, out, thou strumpet, Fortune! All you gods,   475
In general synod, take away her power;
Break all the spokes and fellies from her wheel,
And bowl the round nave down the hill of heaven,
As low as to the fiends."

  Pol. This is too long.   480
  Ham. It shall to the barber's, with your beard. Prithee say
on. He 's for a jig, or a tale of bawdry, or he sleeps. Say
on; come to Hecuba.
  First Play. "But who, ah, who had seen the mobled
    queen—"
  Ham. "The mobled queen"?   485
  Pol. That 's good; "mobled queen" is good.
  First Play. "Run barefoot up and down, threat'ning the
    flames
With bisson rheum; a clout upon that head
Where late the diadem stood, and for a robe,
About her lank and all o'er teemed loins,   490
A blanket, in the alarm of fear caught up—
Who this had seen, with tongue in venom steep'd,
'Gainst Fortune's state would treason have pronounc'd.
But if the gods themselves did see her then,
When she saw Pyrrhus make malicious sport   495
In mincing with his sword her husband's limbs,
The instant burst of clamour that she made—
Unless things mortal move them not at all—
Would have made milch the burning eyes of heaven,
And passion in the gods."   500
  Pol. Look whe'er he has not turn'd his colour, and has
tears in 's eyes. Prithee no more.

467. **orb:** globe of the earth.

469. **region:** the whole space of air; the skies.

471. **Cyclops:** The Cyclopes, huge monsters with a single eye set in the middle of the forehead, were the traditional workmen of Vulcan, the Roman god who forged the armour of Mars, the war god.

472. **for proof eterne:** for everlasting invulnerability. *Proof* denoted the resisting power of armour.

477. **fellies:** the separate arcs of a wheel rim. Fortune is usually represented as blindfolded and turning a wheel, to signify "that she is turning, and inconstant, and mutability, and variation". (Henry V, III. vi. 34.)

478. **nave:** hub.

482. **jig:** a dance, or an interlude of a lively, comic or even farcical kind, given at the end, or in the interval, of a play.

484. **mobled:** muffled. Has the phrase struck some chord of association with Hamlet's mother, possibly veiled in mourning?

488. **bisson rheum:** blinding tears.

490. **o'er teemed:** exhausted by child bearing. According to legend, Hecuba was mother of fifty sons and fifty daughters.

492. **Who this had seen:** anyone who saw this.

493. **state:** power.

499. **milch:** literally *giving milk*. Here, it means *moist*, or *tearful*.

Ham. 'Tis well; I' ll have thee speak out the rest of this soon.—Good my lord, will you see the players well bestowed?   Do you hear: let them be well used; for they are the abstract and brief chronicles of the time; after your death you were better have a bad epitaph than their ill report while you live.   508

Pol. My lord, I will use them according to their desert.

Ham. God's bodykins, man, much better.   Use every man after his desert, and who shall scape whipping?   Use them after your own honour and dignity: the less they deserve, the more merit is in your bounty.   Take them in.   513

Pol. Come, sirs.

Ham. Follow him, friends.   We 'll hear a play to-morrow. Dost thou hear me, old friend; can you play "The Murder of Gonzago"?

First Play. Ay, my lord.   518

Ham. We 'll ha 't to-morrow night.   You could, for a need, study a speech of some dozen or sixteen lines which I would set down and insert in 't, could you not?

First Play. Ay, my lord.   522

Ham. Very well.   Follow that lord; and look you mock him not.   [*Exeunt* POLONIUS *and* PLAYERS.]   My good friends, I 'll leave you till night.   You are welcome to Elsinore.

Ros. Good my lord!

[*Exeunt* ROSENCRANTZ *and* GUILDENSTERN.

Ham. Ay, so God buy to you!   Now I am alone.
O, what a rogue and peasant slave am I!
Is it not monstrous that this player here,   530
But in a fiction, in a dream of passion,
Could force his soul so to his own conceit
That from her working all his visage wann'd;
Tears in his eyes, distraction in 's aspect,
A broken voice, and his whole function suiting   535
With forms to his conceit?   And all for nothing!
For Hecuba!
What 's Hecuba to him or he to Hecuba,

505. **bestowed**: lodged.

510. **bodykins**: diminutive form of *body*.

512. **after**: according to; in a manner befitting.

523-4. **mock him not**: Hamlet does not want the actors to copy his own treatment of Polonius.

532. **conceit**: imagination.
533. **her**: *i.e.* his soul's. **wann'd**: went pale.

535. **function**: the working of the faculties.
536. **forms**: manners, gestures, and facial expressions.

That he should weep for her? What would he do,
Had he the motive and the cue for passion   540
That I have?   He would drown the stage with tears,
And cleave the general ear with horrid speech;
Make mad the guilty, and appal the free,
Confound the ignorant, and amaze indeed
The very faculties of eyes and ears.   545
Yet I,
A dull and muddy-mettl'd rascal, peak,
Like John-a-dreams, unpregnant of my cause,
And can say nothing; no, not for a king
Upon whose property and most dear life   550
A damn'd defeat was made.   Am I a coward?
Who calls me villain, breaks my pate across,
Plucks off my beard and blows it in my face,
Tweaks me by the nose, gives me the lie i' th' throat
As deep as to the lungs? Who does me this?   555
Ha!
'S wounds, I should take it; for it cannot be
But I am pigeon-liver'd and lack gall
To make oppression bitter, or ere this
I should 'a fatted all the region kites   560
With this slave's offal. Bloody, bawdy villain!
Remorseless, treacherous, lecherous, kindless villain!
O, vengeance!
Why, what an ass am I! This is most brave,
That I, the son of a dear father murder'd,   565
Prompted to my revenge by heaven and hell,
Must, like a whore, unpack my heart with words,
And fall a-cursing like a very drab,
A scullion! Fie upon 't! foh!
About, my brains. Hum—I have heard   570
That guilty creatures, sitting at a play,
Have by the very cunning of the scene
Been struck so to the soul that presently
They have proclaim'd their malefactions;
For murder, though it have no tongue, will speak   575
With most miraculous organ. I 'll have these players

542. **cleave the general ear:** split the ears of the groundlings and "general public".

543. **free:** innocent.

546 Muddy - mettled = mean spirited.

547. **peak:** pine; waste away.

548. **John-a-dreams:** Dreamy John. No special reference can be found, but the meaning is obvious. **unpregnant of my cause:** not stirred by, inactive in, my duty.

550. **property:** everything he possessed, including wife and position.

551. **defeat:** destruction; ruin.

554-5. **gives me the lie . . . lungs:** This would be to accuse Hamlet of lying in the most insulting terms.

557. **'S wounds:** By God's wounds (the wounds suffered by Christ on the Cross). **take it:** accept without a murmur.

558 But - Herwise than

558. **pigeon-liver'd:** Pigeons and doves were supposed to secrete no gall, which was thought to be the physical source of courage and spite.

560. **region:** "of the air", as in line 469.

562. **kindless:** devoid of human nature; unnatural.

567. **with words:** *i.e.* instead of actions.

570. **About, my brains:** Wits, to your work.

572. **cunning:** skill.

573. **presently:** immediately; at once.

576. **organ:** instrument.

Play something like the murder of my father
Before mine uncle. I 'll observe his looks;
I 'll tent him to the quick. If 'a do blench,
I know my course. The spirit that I have seen   580
May be a devil; and the devil hath power
T' assume a pleasing shape; yea and perhaps
Out of my weakness and my melancholy,
As he is very potent with such spirits,
Abuses me to damn me. I 'll have grounds   585
More relative than this. The play 's the thing
Wherein I 'll catch the conscience of the King.   [*Exit.*

579. **tent:** probe. A *tent* was a roll of linen for probing a wound. **blench:** flinch (from the probing).

581. **the devil hath power:** Sir Thomas Browne's *Religio Medici* is often quoted to show that it was a fairly general belief that ghosts were really devils in disguise. Some see this as the root of Hamlet's problem, but if so, it comes rather late in the soliloquy (and, indeed, the play). The trend of thought in the speech seems to be that Hamlet finds himself unable to act directly, and the "mousetrap" is a device to provide action of some sort, and perhaps it will force Claudius's hand, or even Hamlet's own.

584. **such spirits:** *i.e.* Hamlet's low spirits—his weakness of mind and his melancholy.

585. **Abuses:** deludes; deceives.

586. **relative:** conclusive.

ACT III

Scene I. *Elsinore. The Castle.*

Enter KING, QUEEN, POLONIUS, OPHELIA, ROSENCRANTZ,
and GUILDENSTERN.

King. And can you by no drift of conference
Get from him why he puts on this confusion,
Grating so harshly all his days of quiet
With turbulent and dangerous lunacy?
Ros. He does confess he feels himself distracted,   5
But from what cause 'a will by no means speak.
Guil. Nor do we find him forward to be sounded;
But, with a crafty madness, keeps aloof
When we would bring him on to some confession
Of his true state.
Queen.   Did he receive you well?   10
Ros. Most like a gentleman.
Guil. But with much forcing of his disposition.
Ros. Niggard of question; but of our demands
Most free in his reply.
Queen.   Did you assay him
To any pastime?   15
Ros. Madam, it so fell out that certain players
We o'er-raught on the way. Of these we told him;
And there did seem in him a kind of joy
To hear of it. They are here about the court,
And, as I think, they have already order   20
This night to play before him.
Pol.   'Tis most true;
And he beseech'd me to entreat your Majesties
To hear and see the matter.
King. With all my heart; and it doth much content me
To hear him so inclin'd.   25

ACT III. SCENE I

1. **drift of conference**: leading him on in conversation.

3. **Grating**: vexing.

8. **keeps aloof**: maintains a reserve.

12. **forcing of his disposition**: constraint in his manner.
13-14. **Niggard of question . . . reply**: Not inclined to converse but ready to answer our questions. The two courtiers are concealing from Claudius and Gertrude the fact that they had failed in their mission by being detected at once by Hamlet, and trying to create a good impression of the interview they had.
14. **assay him**: try to interest him in.

17. **o'er-raught**: over-reached; overtook.

Good gentlemen, give him a further edge,
And drive his purpose into these delights.
   Ros. We shall, my lord.
               [*Exeunt* ROSENCRANTZ *and* GUILDENSTERN.
   King.   Sweet Gertrude, leave us too;
For we have closely sent for Hamlet hither,
That he, as 'twere by accident, may here   30
Affront Ophelia.
Her father and myself—lawful espials—
Will so bestow ourselves that, seeing unseen,
We may of their encounter frankly judge,
And gather by him, as he is behav'd,   35
If 't be th' affliction of his love or no
That thus he suffers for.
   Queen.   I shall obey you;
And for your part, Ophelia, I do wish
That your good beauties be the happy cause
Of Hamlet's wildness; so shall I hope your virtues   40
Will bring him to his wonted way again,
To both your honours.
   Oph.   Madam, I wish it may.
                   [*Exit* QUEEN.
   Pol. Ophelia, walk you here.—Gracious, so please you,
We will bestow ourselves.—Read on this book;
That show of such an exercise may colour   45
Your loneliness.—We are oft to blame in this:
'Tis too much prov'd, that with devotion's visage
And pious action we do sugar o'er
The devil himself.
   King. [*Aside.*] O, 'tis too true!
How smart a lash that speech doth give my conscience! 50
The harlot's cheek, beautied with plast'ring art,
Is not more ugly to the thing that helps it
Than is my deed to my most painted word.
O heavy burden!
   Pol. I hear him coming; let 's withdraw, my lord. 55
               [*Exeunt* KING *and* POLONIUS.
          Enter HAMLET.

26. **give him a further edge:** whet his keenness. These lines are a fine example of dramatic irony.

29. **closely:** secretly; privately.

31. **Affront:** confront; encounter.
32. **espials:** spies.

34. **frankly:** unrestrictedly; without restraint (from Hamlet's "antic disposition").

45. **exercise:** the usual word for an act of devotion. The book, therefore, is probably a prayer book. **colour:** to disguise; hide the real purpose of.

52. **to the thing that helps it:** compared with what beautifies it. These lines, 50-4, are the first signs of repentance, or even real guilt, in Claudius, and prepare us for the prayer scene.

Ham. To be, or not to be--that is the question;
Whether 'tis nobler in the mind to suffer
The slings and arrows of outrageous fortune,
Or to take arms against a sea of troubles,
And by opposing end them? To die, to sleep—   60
No more; and by a sleep to say we end
The heart-ache and the thousand natural shocks
That flesh is heir to. 'Tis a consummation
Devoutly to be wish'd. To die, to sleep;
To sleep, perchance to dream. Ay, there 's the rub;   65
For in that sleep of death what dreams may come,
When we have shuffled off this mortal coil,
Must give us pause. There 's the respect
That makes calamity of so long life;
For who would bear the whips and scorns of time,   70
Th' oppressor's wrong, the proud man's contumely,
The pangs of despis'd love, the law's delay,
The insolence of office, and the spurns
That patient merit of th' unworthy takes,
When he himself might his quietus make   75
With a bare bodkin? Who would these fardels bear,
To grunt and sweat under a weary life,
But that the dread of something after death—
The undiscover'd country, from whose bourn
No traveller returns—puzzles the will,   80
And makes us rather bear those ills we have
Than fly to others that we know not of?
Thus conscience does make cowards of us all;
And thus the native hue of resolution
Is sicklied o'er with the pale cast of thought,   85
And enterprises of great pitch and moment,
With this regard, their currents turn awry
And lose the name of action.—Soft you now!
The fair Ophelia.—Nymph, in thy orisons
Be all my sins rememb'red.
Oph.   Good my lord,   90
How does your honour for this many a day?
Ham. I humbly thank you; well, well, well.

56. **To be, or not to be:** There is ambiguity here, with the following senses: (1) "Is my proposed act of revenge to be or not?" *i.e.* "Shall I act or not?" This question is then expanded more clearly in the next few lines, and the idea of "to die" is suggested by the words "end them". (2) "Shall I go on living or not?" *i.e.* Hamlet contemplates suicide. In this case, the following lines either (*a*) mean that he is setting aside these two possibly nobler courses ("to suffer" and "to take arms") as irrelevant to his central question (*i.e.* whether means *even if*), or (*b*) are a short-lived attempt to shy away from the dreadful idea of suicide (for God has "fix'd his canon 'gainst self slaughter") by pretending to himself that he really meant, "Shall I suffer or take arms?"

In fact, this ambiguity, coming as it does from a play so full of quibbles and double-meanings, is probably deliberate. Hamlet is aware of his problem, but not of its true nature, and Shakespeare indicates this confusion in the mind of the hero with a question which can include most of the possibilities Hamlet is faced with.

58. **slings:** *i.e.* sling shots.

59. **to take arms against a sea:** editors have felt this to be a badly mixed metaphor, and have attempted emendations. Celtic legends are quoted of actual battles with the sea, but there seems little real difficulty, if we accept *sea* in the sense of *innumerable waves* or *host*.

61. **No more:** "it is no more than that".

65. **rub:** difficulty. The metaphor is from bowls, a *rub* being an inequality in the green which diverts the bowl from its proper course.

67. **mortal coil:** the turmoil and anxieties of our mortal life. Though many would disagree, it seems probable that there is also a quibbling reference to *shuffling* the feet to get out of a coil of rope encircling the body. *Coil* in this latter sense is only found written down in 1627, but this is not conclusive evidence that the word did not exist earlier.

68. **respect:** consideration.

69. **of so long life:** so long lived.

70-4. **who would bear . . . takes:** Several critics have pointed out Hamlet's ability to generalise a situation, ignoring his personal involvement. Of these lines, Johnson comments, "Hamlet . . . forgets, whether properly or not, that he is a prince, and mentions many evils to which inferior stations only are exposed". Another speculative generalisation can be found at I. IV. 23-38.

71. **contumely:** contempt.

73. **office:** *i.e.* those in office.

74. **That patient merit . . . takes:** which the patient, virtuous man suffers at the hands of the unworthy.

75. **quietus make:** settle all accounts.

76. **a bare bodkin:** a mere dagger, *not* a naked dagger. **fardels:** burdens.

79. **bourn:** boundary; limit. Has Hamlet momentarily forgotten the ghost, or is this a sign that he no longer believes it to be a ghost, but a devil?

83. **conscience:** consciousness; reflection; reasoning.

85. **thought:** anxiety; melancholy thought.

86. **pitch:** height. The term is from hawking, used to describe the highest point of a falcon's flight.

89. **The fair Ophelia:** Hamlet has been sent for secretly by the King

Oph. My lord, I have remembrances of yours
That I have longed long to re-deliver.
I pray you now receive them.

Ham.   No, not I;   95
I never gave you aught.

Oph. My honour'd lord, you know right well you did,
And with them words of so sweet breath compos'd
As made the things more rich; their perfume lost,
Take these again; for to the noble mind   100
Rich gifts wax poor when givers prove unkind.
There, my lord.

Ham. Ha, ha! Are you honest?

Oph. My lord?

Ham. Are you fair?   105

Oph. What means your lordship?

Ham. That if you be honest and fair, your honesty should
admit no discourse to your beauty.

Oph. Could beauty, my lord, have better commerce than
with honesty?   110

Ham. Ay, truly; for the power of beauty will sooner
transform honesty from what it is to a bawd than the force
of honesty can translate beauty into his likeness. This was
sometime a paradox, but now the time gives it proof. I did
love you once.   115

Oph. Indeed, my lord, you made me believe so.

Ham. You should not have believ'd me; for virtue cannot
so inoculate our old stock but we shall relish of it. I loved
you not.

Oph. I was the more deceived.   120

Ham. Get thee to a nunnery. Why wouldst thou be a
breeder of sinners? I am myself indifferent honest, but yet
I could accuse me of such things that it were better my
mother had not borne me: I am very proud, revengeful,
ambitious; with more offences at my beck than I have thoughts
to put them in, imagination to give them shape, or time to act
them in. What should such fellows as I do crawling between
earth and heaven? We are arrant knaves, all; believe none
of us. Go thy ways to a nunnery. Where 's your father?

(line 29); he meets Ophelia, to whom access has been denied him. Does he therefore suspect a trap? He easily detected the plan with regard to Rosencrantz and Guildenstern; why should he not be equally penetrating here? Alternatively, see note at II. ii. 167. It seems certain that by line 129 Hamlet is aware of the listeners, with his question about Polonius's whereabouts. **orisons: prayers.** During Hamlet's soliloquy, Ophelia has probably been at prayer, probably on the inner stage or "study".

96. **I never gave you aught:** Hamlet means that he was a different man when he gave her the presents. It is possible, however, that Hamlet, feigning madness, is pretending not to know Ophelia.

101. **givers prove unkind:** J. Dover Wilson points out that it was Ophelia who was told to break with Hamlet. This, together with the "coincidence" of Ophelia's presence, chancing to have with her Hamlet's gifts, is possibly why the Prince suspects a trap.

103. **honest:** chaste.

108. **admit no discourse to:** "allow no one to converse with". Ophelia, however, interprets the phrase more narrowly as "refuse to converse with".

109. **commerce:** conversation.

113. **translate:** transform.

114. **sometime:** once. **the time gives it proof:** *i.e.* the present age shows it to be true. Hamlet is referring to the conduct of his mother as well as of Ophelia, whose beauty is here being used dishonestly as bait in Polonius's trap.

116. **relish of it:** retain the flavour of the old stock. The metaphor is from the grafting (*inoculation*) of one fruit tree upon another. *Our old stock* is another oblique reference to Hamlet's mother. Ophelia should not have believed him because he is of the same stock as the inconstant Queen. **I loved you not:** Hamlet means that either he or she has changed so much as to be a different person.

122. **indifferent:** fairly.

124-5. **I am very . . . ambitious:** either Hamlet, in the bitterness of his spirit, is carrying his self-condemnation too far, or perhaps these words are ironical, for certainly everything we know shows that they are the reverse of the truth: his most intimate friend is the humble student, Horatio, and he even extends the name of friend to an actor; he has a terrible vengeance imposed upon him and yet hesitates to exact it; he was anxious to return to Wittenberg. Another possible explanation of the words is that Hamlet expects them to be carried to Claudius, whom they will frighten. (See also line 147.)

129. **Where 's your father:** clearly, now, Hamlet suspects not only a trap, but also that Polonius is eavesdropping.

Oph. At home, my lord.   130
Ham. Let the doors be shut upon him, that he may play
the fool nowhere but in 's own house. Farewell.
Oph. O, help him, you sweet heavens!   133
Ham. If thou dost marry, I 'll give thee this plague for
thy dowry: be thou as chaste as ice, as pure as snow, thou
shalt not escape calumny. Get thee to a nunnery, go, fare-
well. Or, if thou wilt needs marry, marry a fool; for wise
men know well enough what monsters you make of them.
To a nunnery, go; and quickly too. Farewell.
Oph. O heavenly powers, restore him!   140
Ham. I have heard of your paintings too, well enough;
God hath given you one face, and you make yourselves
another. You jig and amble, and you lisp, and nickname
God's creatures, and make your wantonness your ignorance.
Go to, I 'll no more on 't; it hath made me mad. I say we
will have no moe marriage: those that are married already,
all but one, shall live; the rest shall keep as they are. To a
nunnery, go.   [*Exit.*
Oph. O, what a noble mind is here o'erthrown!
The courtier's, soldier's, scholar's, eye, tongue, sword;   150
Th' expectancy and rose of the fair state,
The glass of fashion and the mould of form,
Th' observ'd of all observers—quite, quite down!
And I, of ladies most deject and wretched,
That suck'd the honey of his music vows,   155
Now see that noble and most sovereign reason,
Like sweet bells jangled, out of time and harsh;
That unmatch'd form and feature of blown youth
Blasted with ecstasy. O, woe is me
T' have seen what I have seen, see what I see!   160

Re-enter KING *and* POLONIUS.

King. Love! His affections do not that way tend;
Nor what he spake, though it lack'd form a little,
Was not like madness. There 's something in his soul
O'er which his melancholy sits on brood;
And I do doubt the hatch and the disclose   165

130. **At home:** obviously a deliberate lie, but how else could she answer—especially to a madman?

138. **monsters:** *i.e.* cuckolds, who are always described as having horns.

143. **jig:** walk as if dancing a jig.
143-4. **nickname ... ignorance:** you misname things in wanton fashion, and pretend the ignorance of innocence as an excuse for your wantonness.

146. **moe:** more.
147. **all but one:** *i.e.* the King. Again, this is meant to reach the ears of Claudius.

151. **Th' expectancy . . . state:** hope and chief ornament of the state, which his presence makes fair. For the proleptic use of *fair*, cp. "purged the gentle weal" (*Macbeth*, III. iv. 76), *i.e.* "made the state gentle by purging it".
152. **The glass . . . form:** men copied his dress, and modelled their behaviour on his.

158. **feature:** the whole figure, not merely the face or part of the face, **blown youth:** youth like a flower in full bloom.
159. **ecstasy:** madness.

161. **affections:** emotions; feelings.

164. **on brood:** brooding.
165. **disclose:** disclosure, which almost repeats *hatch*, used here for the opening of the shell.

HAM. 5

Will be some danger; which to prevent
I have in quick determination
Thus set it down: he shall with speed to England
For the demand of our neglected tribute.
Haply the seas and countries different,   170
With variable objects, shall expel
This something-settled matter in his heart
Whereon his brains still beating puts him thus
From fashion of himself. What think you on 't?
   Pol. It shall do well. But yet do I believe   175
The origin and commencement of his grief
Sprung from neglected love. How now, Ophelia!
You need not tell us what Lord Hamlet said;
We heard it all. My lord, do as you please;
But if you hold it fit, after the play   180
Let his queen mother all alone entreat him
To show his grief. Let her be round with him;
And I 'll be placed, so please you, in the ear
Of all their conference. If she find him not,
To England send him; or confine him where   185
Your wisdom best shall think.
   King.   It shall be so:
Madness in great ones must not unwatch'd go.   [*Exeunt.*

SCENE II. *Elsinore. The Castle.*

Enter HAMLET *and three of the* PLAYERS.

   Ham. Speak the speech, I pray you, as I pronounc'd it to you, trippingly on the tongue; but if you mouth it, as many of our players do, I had as lief the town-crier spoke my lines. Nor do not saw the air too much with your hand, thus, but use all gently; for in the very torrent, tempest, and, as I may say, whirlwind of your passion, you must acquire and beget a temperance that may give it smoothness. O, it offends me to the soul to hear a robustious periwig-pated fellow tear a passion to tatters, to very rags, to split the ears of the groundlings, who, for the most part, are capable of nothing but inexplicable dumb shows and noise. I would have such a fellow

166. **prevent**: anticipate.
167. **determination**: decision.

171. **variable objects**: *i.e.* variety of objects.
172. **something-settled**: rather well-established.
173. **his brains still beating**: this is equivalent to "the beating of his brains".
174. **fashion of himself**: his usual habits.

180. **hold**: consider.

182. **his grief**: *i.e.* the cause of his grief.

184. **find him**: detect what is wrong with him.

ACT III, SCENE II

1. **Speak the speech**: These lines of acute critical comment are not really a digression: they prepare us for the play to come, relieve for a moment the tragic tension, and give further proof of Hamlet's sanity. (See also Introduction, p. 22.)
2. **mouth**: rant.
3. **I had as lief**: I would like it as much as if.

7. **temperance**: moderation; restraint.
8. **robustious**: violent. **periwig-pated**: in those days, only actors wore wigs.
9. **groundlings**: the occupants of the theatre corresponding to the modern pit, generally called the "yard", surrounding the stage (see Introduction, p. 3). Gibes at the inferior understanding of the groundlings were fairly common in Elizabethan plays.
10. **capable of**: able to appreciate. **inexplicable**: senseless; unintelligible

whipp'd for o'erdoing Termagant; it out-herods Herod. Pray
you avoid it.   13
   First Play. I warrant your honour.
   Ham. Be not too tame neither, but let your own discretion be your tutor. Suit the action to the word, the word to
the action; with this special observance, that you o'erstep not
the modesty of nature; for anything so o'erdone is from the
purpose of playing, whose end, both at the first and now, was
and is to hold, as 'twere, the mirror up to nature; to show
virtue her own feature, scorn her own image, and the very
age and body of the time his form and pressure. Now, this
overdone or come tardy off, though it makes the unskilful
laugh, cannot but make the judicious grieve; the censure of
the which one must, in your allowance, o'erweigh a whole
theatre of others. O, there be players that I have seen play
—and heard others praise, and that highly—not to speak it
profanely, that, neither having th' accent of Christians, nor
the gait of Christian, pagan, nor man, have so strutted and
bellowed that I have thought some of Nature's journeymen
had made men, and not made them well, they imitated
humanity so abominably.   32
   First Play. I hope we have reform'd that indifferently
with us, sir.
   Ham. O reform it altogether. And let those that play
your clowns speak no more than is set down for them; for
there be of them that will themselves laugh, to set on some
quantity of barren spectators ·to laugh too, though in the
meantime some necessary question of the play be then to
be considered. That 's villainous, and shows a most pitiful
ambition in the fool that uses it. Go, make you ready.   41
                                            [Exeunt PLAYERS.

    Enter POLONIUS, ROSENCRANTZ, *and* GUILDENSTERN.

How now, my lord! Will the King hear this piece of work?
   Pol. And the Queen too, and that presently.
   Ham. Bid the players make haste.   *[Exit* POLONIUS.
Will you two help to hasten them?   45
   Ros. Ay, my lord.   *[Exeunt they two.*

12. **Termagant . . . Herod:** These were stock characters in the old Mystery plays, both being represented as violent and ranting. Termagant was an imaginary deity of the Saracens, often linked with Mahound (Mahomet). Herod was the typical furious tyrant, a braggart and a boaster.

18. **modesty:** moderation. **from:** away from; foreign to.

22. **pressure:** impression; character.
23. **come tardy off:** feebly represented.

25. **allowance:** opinion; estimate.

28. **profanely:** the profanity lies in the allusion to *Nature's journeymen* in line 30. It might be thought a slight on God's handiwork.
30. **journeymen:** men who worked by the day, and who were therefore not very careful.

33. **indifferently:** fairly well.

36. **your clowns:** Shakespeare is complaining here of a practice common at the time, of introducing extempore material into their parts. Some think the complaint an attack on William Kemp who left Shakespeare's company at about the time when *Hamlet* was written, to join a rival company.

42. **piece of work:** masterpiece. Hamlet uses the phrase ironically.
43. **presently:** immediately.

Ham. What, ho, Horatio!

Enter HORATIO.

   Hor. Here, sweet lord, at your service.
   Ham. Horatio, thou art e'en as just a man
As e'er my conversation cop'd withal.   50
   Hor. O, my dear lord!
   Ham.   Nay, do not think I flatter;
For what advancement may I hope from thee,
That no revenue hast but thy good spirits
To feed and clothe thee?   Why should the poor be flatter'd?
No, let the candied tongue lick absurd pomp,   55
And crook the pregnant hinges of the knee
Where thrift may follow fawning.   Dost thou hear?
Since my dear soul was mistress of her choice
And could of men distinguish her election,
Sh' hath seal'd thee for herself; for thou hast been   60
As one, in suff'ring all, that suffers nothing;
A man that Fortune's buffets and rewards
Hast ta'en with equal thanks; and blest are those
Whose blood and judgment are so well comeddled
That they are not a pipe for Fortune's finger   65
To sound what stop she please.   Give me that man
That is not passion's slave, and I will wear him
In my heart's core, ay, in my heart of heart,
As I do thee.   Something too much of this.
There is a play to-night before the King;   70
One scene of it comes near the circumstance
Which I have told thee of my father's death.
I prithee, when thou seest that act afoot,
Even with the very comment of thy soul
Observe my uncle.   If his occulted guilt   75
Do not itself unkennel in one speech,
It is a damned ghost that we have seen,
And my imaginations are as foul
As Vulcan's stithy.   Give him heedful note;
For I mine eyes will rivet to his face;   8o
And, after, we will both our judgments join

49. **just**: honourable; upright.
50. **As e'er . . . withal**: as ever I conversed with.

55. **candied**: sugared, both with flattering words and with the sweet-meats they have earned. The first image is of a dog licking the hand of *pomp*, which suggests the courtiers bending their *knees*, which turns the attention back to the dog fawning round the knees of pomp, this time in hope of gain (*thrift*).
56. **pregnant**: ready; prompt.
59. **of men**: between men. **election**: choice.

64. **blood and judgment**: passion and reason. The blood was once supposed to be the seat of the passions. **comeddled**: intermingled; mixed.

74. **comment of thy soul**: the closest observation your soul is capable of.
75. **occulted**: hidden.
76. **in one speech**: *i.e.* the one which Hamlet has written.

79. **Vulcan's stithy**: The smithy of Vulcan, supposed to be under Mount Etna (see note on II. ii. 471). An appropriate image, for Jove's avenging thunderbolts were made there.

In censure of his seeming.
    Hor.   Well, my lord.
If 'a steal aught the whilst this play is playing,
And scape detecting, I will pay the theft.

      Enter trumpets and kettledrums.   Danish march.
                 Sound a flourish.

Enter KING, QUEEN, POLONIUS, OPHELIA, ROSENCRANTZ,
GUILDENSTERN, *and other* LORDS *attendant, with the*
           GUARD *carrying torches.*

    Ham.   They are coming to the play; I must be idle.   85
Get you a place.
    King.   How fares our cousin Hamlet?
    Ham.   Excellent, i' faith; of the chameleon's dish. I eat
the air, promise-cramm'd; you cannot feed capons so.
    King.   I have nothing with this answer, Hamlet; these
words are not mine.   91
    Ham.   No, nor mine now. [*To* POLONIUS.]   My lord,
you play'd once i' th' university, you say?
    Pol.   That did I, my lord, and was accounted a good actor.
    Ham.   What did you enact?   95
    Pol.   I did enact Julius Caesar; I was kill'd i' th' Capitol;
Brutus kill'd me.
    Ham.   It was a brute part of him to kill so capital a calf
there. Be the players ready?
    Ros.   Ay, my lord; they stay upon your patience.   100
    Queen.   Come hither, my dear Hamlet, sit by me.
    Ham.   No, good mother; here 's metal more attractive.
    Pol.   [*To the* KING.]   O, ho! do you mark that?
    Ham.   Lady, shall I lie in your lap?
                         [*Lying down at* OPHELIA'S *feet.*
    Oph.   No, my lord.   105
    Ham.   I mean, my head upon your lap?
    Oph.   Ay, my lord.
    Ham.   Do you think I meant country matters?
    Oph.   I think nothing, my lord.
    Ham.   That 's a fair thought to lie between maids' legs.
    Oph.   What is, my lord?   111

82. **censure of his seeming**: assessing his appearance (of guilt).

85. **idle**: *i.e.* put on his "antic disposition".

88. **of the chameleon's dish**: Hamlet quibbles with *fares*, taking it as *eats*, and replies that he feeds on air, which is what the chameleon was popularly supposed to live on.   J. Dover Wilson points out that *air* is a quibble on *heir*, and that this is another hint at thwarted ambition.

89. **promise-cramm'd**: alludes to the King's remarks in I. ii.   To be called a *capon* was to be a fool, so that Hamlet means finally that even a fool would not be fed on the air of such promises.

93. **play'd once i' th' university**: plays, both in Latin and English, were performed at Oxford and Cambridge in Shakespeare's day.

96. **th' Capitol**: This popular error as to the place of Caesar's death is repeated by Shakespeare in *Julius Caesar*.

100. **stay upon your patience**: await your readiness.

104. **lie in your lap**: Hamlet's obscenity here is a continuation of the insults he heaped upon Ophelia in the previous scene.   He will make her suffer for her part in that plot.

108. **country matters**: immoral behaviour.

Ham. Nothing.

Oph. You are merry, my lord.

Ham. Who, I?

Oph. Ay, my lord.   115

Ham. O God, your only jig-maker! What should a man
do but be merry? For look you how cheerfully my mother
looks, and my father died within 's two hours.

Oph. Nay, 'tis twice two months, my lord.   119

Ham. So long? Nay then, let the devil wear black, for
I 'll have a suit of sables. O heavens! die two months ago,
and not forgotten yet? Then there 's hope a great man's
memory may outlive his life half a year; but by 'r lady, 'a
must build churches, then; or else shall 'a suffer not thinking
on, with the hobby-horse, whose epitaph is "For O, for O,
the hobby-horse is forgot!".   126

*The trumpet sounds. Hautboys play. The Dumb Show enters.
Enter a* KING *and a* QUEEN, *very lovingly; the* QUEEN *embrac-
ing him and he her. She kneels, and makes show of protesta-
tion unto him. He takes her up, and declines his head upon
her neck. He lies him down upon a bank of flowers; she,
seeing him asleep, leaves him. Anon comes in a* FELLOW,
*takes off his crown, kisses it, pours poison in the sleeper's
ears, and leaves him. The* QUEEN *returns; finds the King
dead, and makes passionate action. The* POISONER, *with
some two or three* MUTES, *comes in again, seeming to con-
dole with her. The dead body is carried away. The*
POISONER *woos the* QUEEN *with gifts: she seems harsh awhile,
but in the end accepts his love.   [*Exeunt.*

Oph. What means this, my lord?

Ham. Marry, this is miching mallecho; it means mischief.

Oph. Belike this show imports the argument of the play.

Enter PROLOGUE.

Ham. We shall know by this fellow: the players cannot
keep counsel; they 'll tell all.   131

Oph. Will 'a tell us what this show meant?

Ham. Ay, or any show that you will show him. Be not
you asham'd to show, he 'll not shame to tell you what it
means.   135

116. **your only jig-maker**: I am the only jester. *Jig-maker* means writer of jigs, dances performed by clowns.

121. **a suit of sables**: suits trimmed with sable were common and very gorgeous, often of scarlet cloth. Hamlet possibly means to quibble, however, on *sable* meaning *black*. He also suggests "Then I must be getting old" for in IV. vii. 81, *sables* are described as the dress of "settled age".

124. **suffer not thinking on**: be forgotten.

125. **the hobby-horse**: a figure of a horse strapped round the waist of a man whose feet were concealed by a foot-cloth. It appeared in rural May games and morris-dances. The quotation is from an old ballad which was often referred to in Shakespeare's day.

THE DUMB SHOW. The use of the dumb show is peculiar, and not in accordance with the usage of the English stage, where it dealt with action not represented in the dialogue, or with allegorical moralising on the action.

Critics differ as to why the King was not affected by it. Perhaps he did not understand it, as his question in line 221 suggests—and clearly Ophelia is puzzled in line 127. Dover Wilson prefers to believe that the King is whispering to the Queen about Hamlet's conduct at this point, while others, notably Granville Barker, say that this would dissipate the force of the scene by dividing our interest. Of course, possibly it *does* affect Claudius, but he is able to restrain himself from precipitate action, at least for the moment.

128. **miching mallecho**: secret mischief.

129. **imports the argument**: conveys the subject.

Oph. You are naught, you are naught. I 'll mark the play.
Pro.   *For us, and for our tragedy,*
                 Here stooping to your clemency,
                 We beg your hearing patiently.   [*Exit.*
Ham. Is this a prologue, or the posy of a ring?   140
Oph. 'Tis brief, my lord.
Ham. As woman's love.

Enter the PLAYER KING *and* QUEEN.

P. King.   Full thirty times hath Phœbus' cart gone round
Neptune's salt wash and Tellus' orbed ground,
And thirty dozen moons with borrowed sheen   145
About the world have times twelve thirties been,
Since love our hearts and Hymen did our hands
Unite comutual in most sacred bands.
P. Queen.   So many journeys may the sun and moon
Make us again count o'er ere love be done!   150
But, woe is me, you are so sick of late,
So far from cheer and from your former state,
That I distrust you. Yet, though I distrust,
Discomfort you, my lord, it nothing must;
For women fear too much even as they love,   155
And women's fear and love hold quantity,
In neither aught, or in extremity.
Now, what my love is, proof hath made you know;
And as my love is siz'd, my fear is so.
Where love is great, the littlest doubts are fear;   160
Where little fears grow great, great love grows there.
P. King.   Faith, I must leave thee, love, and shortly too:
My operant powers their functions leave to do;
And thou shalt live in this fair world behind,
Honour'd, belov'd; and haply one as kind   165
For husband shalt thou—
P. Queen.   O, confound the rest!
Such love must needs be treason in my breast.
In second husband let me be accurst!
None wed the second but who kill'd the first.

136. **naught:** naughty; licentious.

140. **posy of a ring:** jingling motto, known as a *posy* (poesy), inscribed on the inner side of a ring.

143. **Full thirty times:** The conventional allusions to mythology in these opening lines set the tone of this interlude, which imitates the earlier Elizabethan tragedies, modelled on Seneca. The rhyme, the stilted diction, and the excessive moralising are typical. **Phoebus' cart:** the chariot of the Sun God.

144. **Neptune:** God of water and so of the sea. **Tellus:** the Roman earth-goddess.

145. **borrowed sheen:** radiance reflected from the sun, and therefore "borrowed".

147. **Hymen:** Goddess of marriage.

153. **distrust:** am anxious for.

156-7. **hold quantity . . . extremity:** they are proportionate, each being either absent or excessive.

158. **proof:** experience.

163. **operant:** active. **leave to do:** cease to discharge their functions.

Ham. That 's wormwood, wormwood.   170
   P. Queen. *The instances that second marriage move*
Are base respects of thrift, but none of love.
A second time I kill my husband dead,
When second husband kisses me in bed.
   P. King. *I do believe you think what now you speak;* 175
But what we do determine oft we break.
Purpose is but the slave to memory,
Of violent birth, but poor validity;
Which now, the fruit unripe, sticks on the tree;
But fall unshaken when they mellow be.   180
Most necessary 'tis that we forget
To pay ourselves what to ourselves is debt.
What to ourselves in passion we propose,
The passion ending, doth the purpose lose.
The violence of either grief or joy   185
Their own enactures with themselves destroy.
Where joy most revels grief doth most lament;
Grief joys, joy grieves, on slender accident.
This world is not for aye; nor 'tis not strange
That even our loves should with our fortunes change;   190
For 'tis a question left us yet to prove,
Whether love lead fortune or else fortune love.
The great man down, you mark his favourite flies;
The poor advanc'd makes friends of enemies.
And hitherto doth love on fortune tend;   195
For who not needs shall never lack a friend,
And who in want a hollow friend doth try,
Directly seasons him his enemy.
But, orderly to end where I begun,
Our wills and fates do so contrary run   200
That our devices still are overthrown;
Our thoughts are ours, their ends none of our own.
So think thou wilt no second husband wed;
But die thy thoughts when thy first lord is dead.
   P. Queen. *Nor earth to me give food, nor heaven light,*
Sport and repose lock from me day and night,   206
To desperation turn my trust and hope,

171. **instances:** motives; causes.
172. **respects of thrift:** considerations of gain.

177-8. **Purpose . . . validity:** Our intentions may be very firm when born, but may lose their strength, depending as they do upon our recollections of the causes which gave rise to them. Some critics say that these lines, 177-204, are those specially written by Hamlet, while others insist that he wrote the speech of Lucianus, lines 243-8. There has been much discussion on the question, but it is pure conjecture and really pointless.
180. **fall:** should be singular; the subject is *purpose*.
181. **Most necessary 'tis:** it is inevitable.

186. **enactures:** resolutions. **destroy:** plural because of the confusion of the subject, *violence*, with *grief and joy*.
188. **on slender accident:** for small event; *i.e.* with little cause.

195. **tend: attend:** wait upon.
196. **who not needs:** whoever is not in need.

198. **seasons him:** matures, ripens him as.

201. **still:** always.

An anchor's cheer in prison be my scope,
Each opposite that blanks the face of joy
Meet what I would have well, and it destroy,   210
Both here and hence pursue me lasting strife,
If, once a widow, ever I be wife!

   Ham.   If she should break it now!

   P. King.   *'Tis deeply sworn.   Sweet, leave me here awhile;*
My spirits grow dull, and fain I would beguile   215
The tedious day with sleep.   [*Sleeps.*

   P. Queen.   *Sleep rock thy brain,*
And never come mischance between us twain!   [*Exit.*

   Ham.   Madam, how like you this play?

   Queen.   The lady doth protest too much, methinks.

   Ham.   O, but she 'll keep her word.   220

   King.   Have you heard the argument?   Is there no offence
in 't?

   Ham.   No, no; they do but jest, poison in jest; no offence
i' th' world.

   King.   What do you call the play?   225

   Ham.   "The Mouse-trap."   Marry, how?   Tropically.
This play is the image of a murder done in Vienna:
Gonzago is the duke's name; his wife, Baptista.   You
shall see anon. 'Tis a knavish piece of work; but what
of that?   Your Majesty, and we that have free souls, it
touches us not.   Let the galled jade wince, our withers are
unwrung.   232

Enter LUCIANUS.

This is one Lucianus, nephew to the King.

   Oph.   You are as good as a chorus, my lord.

   Ham.   I could interpret between you and your love, if I
could see the puppets dallying.   236

   Oph.   You are keen, my lord, you are keen.

   Ham.   It would cost you a groaning to take off mine edge.

   Oph.   Still better, and worse.

   Ham.   So you mis-take your husbands.—Begin, murderer;
pox, leave thy damnable faces and begin.   Come; the croaking raven doth bellow for revenge.   242

208. **anchor's cheer:** anchorite's fare. Some explain *cheer* as "chair", quoting a passage from Hall's *Satires*, "Sit seven yeares pining in an anchores cheyre". **scope:** limit.

209. **opposite:** cross; affliction. **blanks:** makes pale.

221. **argument:** plot. **no offence:** Claudius means "nothing capable of giving offence", while Hamlet's ironical reply quibbles with *offence* meaning "crime" or "injury".

226. **Tropically:** "by way of a figure, or trope". Hamlet puns on *trap*, referring to his device to "catch the conscience of the King".

228. **duke's name:** the titles *duke*, *king*, and *count* are not always carefully differentiated in Shakespeare.

230. **free:** innocent.

231. **jade:** a horse in poor condition. **withers:** the junction of the shoulder bones of a horse, forming at the bottom of the neck a ridge which is easily galled by the collar. Hamlet is again being ironic, at the expense of Claudius.

233. **nephew to the King:** Why does not Hamlet say "brother"? Perhaps he is warning Claudius that he is going to exact his revenge.

235. **love;** *i.e.* lover.

236. **the puppets:** at Elizabethan puppet shows an interpreter sat on the stage and explained the action to the audience. Hamlet is again ironic, and also probably making some obscene reference.

237. **keen:** cruel. Cp. our modern phrase "a cutting remark". Hamlet in his reply takes the word to mean "sexually aroused".

239. **better, and worse:** *i.e.* better at being cruel, and with worse indecencies. *Better* also suggests *bitter*.

240. **mis-take:** Ophelia's words, *better and worse*, have suggested the marriage service, in which a woman takes her husband "for better, for worse". The *mis* implies that women are false to their vows.

241-2. **the croaking raven:** the reference is to two lines in *The True Tragedy of Richard the Third:*—

      "The shreeking raven sits croking for revenge,
       Whole herds of beasts come bellowing for revenge."

Hamlet (or Shakespeare) is probably making fun of the ranting player.

Luc. *Thoughts black, hands apt, drugs fit, and time*
    agreeing;
Confederate season, else no creature seeing;
Thou mixture rank, of midnight weeds collected,   245
With Hecat's ban thrice blasted, thrice infected.
Thy natural magic and dire property
On wholesome life usurps immediately.   248

                      [*Pours the poison in his ears.*

Ham. 'A poisons him i' th' garden for his estate. His
name 's Gonzago. The story is extant, and written in very
choice Italian. You shall see anon how the murderer gets
the love of Gonzago's wife.

Oph. The King rises.

Ham. What, frighted with false fire!

Queen. How fares my lord?   255

Pol. Give o'er the play.

King. Give me some light. Away!

Pol. Lights, lights, lights!

              [*Exeunt all but* HAMLET *and* HORATIO.

Ham. Why, let the strucken deer go weep,
    The hart ungalled play;   260
  For some must watch, while some must sleep;
    Thus runs the world away.
Would not this, sir, and a forest of feathers—if the rest of
my fortunes turn Turk with me—with two Provincial roses
on my raz'd shoes, get me a fellowship in a cry of players,
sir?

Hor. Half a share.

Ham. A whole one, I.
    For thou dost know, O Damon dear,
    This realm dismantled was   270
    Of Jove himself; and now reigns here
    A very, very—peacock.

Hor. You might have rhym'd.

Ham. O good Horatio, I 'll take the ghost's word for a
thousand pound. Didst perceive?   275

Hor. Very well, my lord.

Ham. Upon the talk of the poisoning.

244. **Confederate:** conspiring; favouring.

245. **midnight weeds:** *i.e.* herbs collected at midnight, which were essential ingredients of witches' charms and potions. The Weird Sisters' caldron in *Macbeth*, III. i, contained "Root of hemlock digg'd i' the dark" and "slips of yew sliver'd in the moon's eclipse".

246. **Hecat:** a mysterious deity, probably of eastern origin, usually identified with witchcraft in Elizabethan literature, e.g. *Macbeth*.

248. **wholesome:** healthy. **usurps:** encroaches.

250. **The story is extant:** Shakespeare's authority has never been discovered, though Dowden writes, without mentioning a source, "in 1538 a Duke of Urbino, who was married to a Gonzaga, was murdered by one Luigi Gonzaga, who dropped poison into his ear".

254. **false fire:** a metaphor from the discharge of artillery loaded without ball. Hamlet exults that Claudius should shrink from an acted, harmless version of a crime he has actually committed.

259. **deer go weep:** It was believed that a wounded deer would retire alone to weep.

263. **a forest of feathers:** elaborately plumed hats were often worn on the stage in Shakespeare's time.

264. **turn Turk:** change completely for the worse. **Provincial roses:** rosettes of ribbon worn on the shoes to hide the laces, looking like *Provencal roses*.

265. **raz'd:** slashed, or cut in patterns. **fellowship**... **cry:** company.

267. **Half a share:** actors had no fixed salaries, but received shares of the profits in accordance with their ability.

270. **dismantled:** stripped.

271. **Of Jove:** from Jove. This refers, of course, to Hamlet's father.

272. **peacock:** instead of *ass*, which would complete the rhyme. The bird had a reputation for lechery in Elizabethan and earlier times, and so to Hamlet is an appropriate name for Claudius.

Hor. I did very well note him.

Ham. Ah, ha! Come, some music. Come, the recorders.
For if the King like not the comedy,   280
Why, then, belike he likes it not, perdy.
Come, some music.

    Re-enter ROSENCRANTZ *and* GUILDENSTERN.

Guil. Good my lord, vouchsafe me a word with you.

Ham. Sir, a whole history.

Guil. The King, sir—   285

Ham. Ay, sir, what of him?

Guil. Is, in his retirement, marvellous distemp'red.

Ham. With drink, sir?

Guil. No, my lord, rather with choler.   289

Ham. Your wisdom should show itself more richer to signify this to his doctor; for for me to put him to his purgation would perhaps plunge him into far more choler.

Guil. Good my lord, put your discourse into some frame, and start not so wildly from my affair.

Ham. I am tame, sir. Pronounce.   295

Guil. The Queen, your mother, in most great affliction of spirit, hath sent me to you.

Ham. You are welcome.   298

Guil. Nay, good my lord, this courtesy is not of the right breed. If it shall please you to make me a wholesome answer, I will do your mother's commandment; if not, your pardon and my return shall be the end of my business.

Ham. Sir, I cannot.

Ros. What, my lord?   304

Ham. Make you a wholesome answer; my wit 's diseas'd. But, sir, such answer as I can make, you shall command: or rather, as you say, my mother. Therefore no more, but to the matter: my mother, you say—

Ros. Then thus she says: your behaviour hath struck her into amazement and admiration.   310

Ham. O wonderful son, that can so stonish a mother! But is there no sequel at the heels of this mother's admiration? Impart.

281. **perdy**: a corruption of *par Dieu*.

287. **distemp'red**: disordered; discomposed. Typically, Hamlet takes the word up in the wrong sense, of *physical* disorder when Guildenstern meant *mental*.

291. **purgation**: a play on the medical and legal senses of the word, the purging of the body and the clearing from the imputation of guilt.
293. **frame**: order.

300. **wholesome**: reasonable.

302. **pardon**: *permission to leave*, as well as *forgiveness*.

310. **admiration**: wonder; astonishment.
311. **stonish**: dismay; bewilder.

Ros. She desires to speak with you in her closet ere you
go to bed.   315

Ham. We shall obey, were she ten times our mother. Have
you any further trade with us?

Ros. My lord, you once did love me.

Ham. And do still, by these pickers and stealers.   319

Ros. Good my lord, what is your cause of distemper?
You do surely bar the door upon your own liberty, if you
deny your griefs to your friend.

Ham. Sir, I lack advancement.

Ros. How can that be, when you have the voice of the
King himself for your succession in Denmark?   325

Ham. Ay, sir, but "While the grass grows"—the proverb
is something musty.

Re-enter the PLAYERS, *with recorders.*

O, the recorders! Let me see one. To withdraw with you
—why do you go about to recover the wind of me, as if you
would drive me into a toil?   330

Guil. O, my lord, if my duty be too bold, my love is too
unmannerly.

Ham. I do not well understand that. Will you play upon
this pipe?

Guil. My lord, I cannot.   335

Ham. I pray you.

Guil. Believe me, I cannot.

Ham. I do beseech you.

Guil. I know no touch of it, my lord.   339

Ham. It is as easy as lying: govern these ventages with
your fingers and thumb, give it breath with your mouth, and it
will discourse most eloquent music. Look you, these are the
stops.

Guil. But these cannot I command to any utterance of
harmony; I have not the skill.   345

Ham. Why, look you now, how unworthy a thing you
make of me! You would play upon me; you would seem
to know my stops; you would pluck out the heart of my
mystery; you would sound me from my lowest note to the

317. **trade with us:** Hamlet is being contemptuous.

319. **pickers and stealers:** *i.e.* hands.

323. **I lack advancement:** another allusion to ambition. This is what Rosencrantz and Guildenstern suspected in III. ii, and Hamlet encourages the latter to go on believing it.

326. **the proverb:** "While the grass grows the steed starves."

329. **recover the wind:** a hunting term meaning to work round to the windward.
330. **toil:** a net or snare.
331-2. **if my duty . . . unmannerly:** if he appears too forward in doing his duty, it is his love that is responsible for his bad manners.

top of my compass; and there is much music, excellent voice, in this little organ, yet cannot you make it speak. 'S blood, do you think I am easier to be play'd on than a pipe? Call me what instrument you will, though you can fret me, yet you cannot play upon me.

Re-enter POLONIUS.

God bless you, sir!   355
   Pol.   My lord, the Queen would speak with you, and presently.
   Ham.   Do you see yonder cloud that 's almost in shape of a camel?
   Pol.   By th' mass, and 'tis like a camel indeed.   360
   Ham.   Methinks it is like a weasel.
   Pol.   It is back'd like a weasel.
   Ham.   Or like a whale?
   Pol.   Very like a whale.   364
   Ham.   Then I will come to my mother by and by. [*Aside.*] They fool me to the top of my bent.—I will come by and by.
   Pol.   I will say so.   [*Exit* POLONIUS.
   Ham.   "By and by" is easily said. Leave me, friends.
                                        [*Exeunt all but* HAMLET.
'Tis now the very witching time of night,   370
When churchyards yawn, and hell itself breathes out
Contagion to this world. Now could I drink hot blood,
And do such bitter business as the day
Would quake to look on. Soft! now to my mother.
O heart, lose not thy nature; let not ever   375
The soul of Nero enter this firm bosom.
Let me be cruel, not unnatural:
I will speak daggers to her, but use none.
My tongue and soul in this be hypocrites—
How in my words somever she be shent,   380
To give them seals never, my soul, consent!   [*Exit.*

353. **fret**: Hamlet means *vex*, but also puns on the meaning of a *bar* on the fingerboard of a musical instrument, by which the fingering is guided.

357. **presently**: immediately.

366. **They fool me to the top of my bent**: they humour me to whatever lengths I go. **bent**: see note to II. ii. 30.

372. **Contagion**: poisonous influence.

375. **nature**: *i.e.* natural feeling.
376. **Nero**: The Emperor Nero had his mother, Agrippina, murdered.

380. **shent**: shamed.
381. **give them seals**: ratify them by acts.

SCENE III. *Elsinore. The Castle.*

Enter KING, ROSENCRANTZ, *and* GUILDENSTERN.

King. I like him not; nor stands it safe with us
To let his madness range. Therefore prepare you;
I your commission will forthwith dispatch,
And he to England shall along with you.
The terms of our estate may not endure   5
Hazard so near 's as doth hourly grow
Out of his brows.
    Guil.   We will ourselves provide.
Most holy and religious fear it is
To keep those many many bodies safe
That live and feed upon your Majesty.   10
    Ros. The single and peculiar life is bound
With all the strength and armour of the mind
To keep itself from noyance; but much more
That spirit upon whose weal depends and rests
The lives of many. The cease of majesty   15
Dies not alone, but like a gulf doth draw
What 's near it with it. It is a massy wheel,
Fix'd on the summit of the highest mount,
To whose huge spokes ten thousand lesser things
Are mortis'd and adjoin'd; which when it falls,   20
Each small annexment, petty consequence,
Attends the boist'rous ruin. Never alone
Did the king sigh, but with a general groan.
    King. Arm you, I pray you, to this speedy voyage;
For we will fetters put about this fear,   25
Which now goes too free-footed.
    Ros.   We will haste us.
        [*Exeunt* ROSENCRANTZ *and* GUILDENSTERN.

Enter POLONIUS.

    Pol. My lord, he 's going to his mother's closet.
Behind the arras I 'll convey myself
To hear the process. I 'll warrant she 'll tax him home;
And, as you said, and wisely was it said,   30

ACT III.   SCENE III

3. **commission**: *i.e.* the document explaining and authorising their mission to the King of England.

5. **terms of our estate**: our position as king.

7. **brows**: threatening looks. The First Folio reads *lunacies*. **provide**: prepare.

11. **single and peculiar life**: the individual, private person, living only for himself.

13. **noyance**: injury.

14. **weal**: welfare.

15. **cease of majesty**: *i.e.* the death of a king.

16. **gulf**: whirlpool.

20. **mortis'd**: *i.e.* fastened like a tenon in a mortise joint.

21. **annexment**: appendage.

23. **a general groan**: the grief of the whole nation.

24. **Arm you**: prepare yourselves.

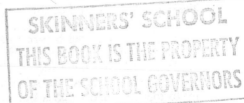

29. **process**: proceedings. **tax him home**: take him to task most thoroughly.

30. **as you said**: Polonius modestly, or forgetfully, assigns his own suggestion to the King.

'Tis meet that some more audience than a mother,
Since nature makes them partial, should o'erhear
The speech, of vantage. Fare you well, my liege.
I 'll call upon you ere you go to bed,
And tell you what I know.
  King.   Thanks, dear my lord. 35
           [*Exit* POLONIUS.
O, my offence is rank, it smells to heaven;
It hath the primal eldest curse upon 't—
A brother's murder! Pray can I not,
Though inclination be as sharp as will.
My stronger guilt defeats my strong intent, 40
And, like a man to double business bound,
I stand in pause where I shall first begin,
And both neglect. What if this cursed hand
Were thicker than itself with brothers' blood,
Is there not rain enough in the sweet heavens 45
To wash it white as snow?   Whereto serves mercy
But to confront the visage of offence?
And what 's in prayer but this twofold force,
To be forestalled ere we come to fall,
Or pardon'd being down?   Then I 'll look up; 50
My fault is past.   But, O, what form of prayer
Can serve my turn?   "Forgive me my foul murder"!
That cannot be; since I am still possess'd
Of those effects for which I did the murder—
My crown, mine own ambition, and my queen. 55
May one be pardon'd and retain th' offence?
In the corrupted currents of this world
Offence's gilded hand may shove by justice;
And oft 'tis seen the wicked prize itself
Buys out the law.   But 'tis not so above: 60
There is no shuffling; there the action lies
In his true nature; and we ourselves compell'd,
Even to the teeth and forehead of our faults,
To give in evidence. What then? What rests?
Try what repentance can. What can it not? 65
Yet what can it when one can not repent?

33. **of vantage**: *i.e.* from a point of vantage.

37. **primal eldest curse**: Cain's murder of his brother, Abel, was the first crime of all.

39. **Though inclination . . . will**: though his desire is as strong as his resolution to pray.

42. **pause**: deliberation.

47. **confront the visage of offence**: to face up to evil.
48. **this twofold force**: prayers can prevent us from sinning, and also obtain pardon if we do err.

56. **th' offence**: *i.e.* the profits of the crime.

59. **the wicked prize itself**: the profits of the crime may be used to buy immunity from justice.
61-2. **the action lies In his true nature**: Claudius is still using legal terms: "There (in Heaven) the legal action is sustainable (*lies*), revealed fully for what it is" (*i.e.* nothing concealed by bribery). There is, however, a more obvious sense, "The deed (act of murder) lies revealed for what it is".
64. **rests**: remains.
65. **can**: is able to do.

O wretched state! O bosom black as death!
O limed soul, that, struggling to be free,
Art more engag'd! Help, angels. Make assay:
Bow, stubborn knees; and, heart, with strings of steel,   70
Be soft as sinews of the new-born babe.
All may be well.   [*Retires and kneels.*

Enter HAMLET.

  Ham. Now might I do it pat, now 'a is a-praying;
And now I 'll do 't—and so 'a goes to heaven,
And so am I reveng'd. That would be scann'd: 75
A villain kills my father; and for that,
I, his sole son, do this same villain send
To heaven.
Why, this is hire and salary, not revenge.
'A took my father grossly, full of bread,   80
With all his crimes broad blown, as flush as May;
And how his audit stands who knows save heaven?
But in our circumstance and course of thought
'Tis heavy with him; and am I then reveng'd
To take him in the purging of his soul,   85
When he is fit and season'd for his passage?
No.
Up, sword, and know thou a more horrid hent.
When he is drunk asleep, or in his rage;
Or in th' incestuous pleasure of his bed;   90
At game, a-swearing, or about some act
That has no relish of salvation in 't—
Then trip him, that his heels may kick at heaven,
And that his soul may be as damn'd and black
As hell, whereto it goes. My mother stays.   95
This physic but prolongs thy sickly days.   [*Exit.*
    King. [*Rising.*] My words fly up, my thoughts remain
           below.
Words without thoughts never to heaven go.   [*Exit.*

68. **limed:** trapped. Birds were often trapped by smearing twigs with a sticky substance called bird-lime.

69. **engag'd:** entangled. **assay:** trial; attempt. The words are probably addressed to the King's soul.

75. **would be scann'd:** needs careful consideration.

79. **hire and salary:** *i.e.* Hamlet would be treating his task as a mere job for pay, and not exacting the full penalty of a personal revenge.

81. **flush:** full of vigour; lusty. Hamlet is here remembering the Ghost's words of I. v. 74-9.

82. **audit:** final reckoning.

83. **in our circumstance . . . thought:** *i.e.* as far as we can judge in our circumstances as mortals.

88. **hent:** intention; design. The O.E.D. quotes a translation of Livy, where *hent* is used for Latin *consilia*. This conclusion has worried the critics, the devout being ready to agree with Dr. Johnson that it is "too horrible to be read or uttered", while others see it as a specious excuse to put off the fateful moment once more. Certainly it is ironic, in view of Claudius's admission that his attempt to pray was unsuccessful.

91. **At game:** *i.e.*, gambling.

95. **stays:** is waiting.

SCENE IV.   *The Queen's closet.*

Enter QUEEN *and* POLONIUS.

Pol. 'A will come straight.   Look you lay home to him;
Tell him his pranks have been too broad to bear with,
And that your Grace hath screen'd and stood between
Much heat and him.   I 'll silence me even here.
Pray you be round with him.
    Ham. [*Within.*]   Mother, mother, mother!   5
    Queen. I 'll warrant you.   Fear me not.
Withdraw, I hear him coming.

                [POLONIUS *goes behind the arras.*

Enter HAMLET.

    Ham. Now, mother, what 's the matter?
    Queen. Hamlet, thou hast thy father much offended.
    Ham. Mother, you have my father much offended.   10
    Queen. Come, come, you answer with an idle tongue.
    Ham. Go, go, you question with a wicked tongue.
    Queen. Why, how now, Hamlet!
    Ham.   What 's the matter now?
    Queen. Have you forgot me?
    Ham.   No, by the rood, not so:
You are the Queen, your husband's brother's wife;   15
And—would it were not so!—you are my mother.
    Queen. Nay then, I 'll set those to you that can speak.
    Ham. Come, come, and sit you down; you shall not budge.
You go not till I set you up a glass
Where you may see the inmost part of you.   20
    Queen. What wilt thou do?   Thou wilt not murder me?
Help, help, ho!
    Pol. [*Behind.*] What, ho! help, help, help!
    Ham. [*Draws.*] How now! a rat?
Dead, for a ducat, dead!   25

      [*Kills* POLONIUS *with a pass through the arras.*
    Pol. [*Behind.*] O, I am slain!
    Queen. O me, what hast thou done?
    Ham.   Nay, I know not:
Is it the King?

ACT III. SCENE IV

5. **round:** straightforward; outspoken.
6. **Fear me not:** have no fears.

9. **thy father:** Gertrude means Claudius, while Hamlet refers in the next line to King Hamlet.
11. **idle:** foolish; careless.

14. **rood:** the Cross.

25. **for a ducat:** I'll wager a ducat.   A *ducat* was a gold coin of varying value, common throughout most of Europe.

Queen. 'O, what a rash and bloody deed is this!
Ham. A bloody deed!—almost as bad, good mother, 30
As kill a king and marry with his brother.
Queen. As kill a king!
Ham. 　　　　　　　　Ay, lady, it was my word.
　　　　　　　　　　　　　　[Parting the arras.
Thou wretched, rash, intruding fool, farewell!
I took thee for thy better. Take thy fortune;
Thou find'st to be too busy is some danger. 35
Leave wringing of your hands. Peace; sit you down,
And let me wring your heart; for so I shall,
If it be made of penetrable stuff;
If damned custom have not braz'd it so
That it be proof and bulwark against sense. 40
Queen. What have I done that thou dar'st wag thy tongue
In noise so rude against me?
Ham. 　　　　　　　　Such an act
That blurs the grace and blush of modesty;
Calls virtue hypocrite; takes off the rose
From the fair forehead of an innocent love, 45
And sets a blister there; makes marriage-vows
As false as dicers' oaths. O, such a deed
As from the body of contraction plucks
The very soul, and sweet religion makes
A rhapsody of words. Heaven's face does glow 50
O'er this solidity and compound mass
With heated visage, as against the doom—
Is thought-sick at the act.
Queen. 　　　　　　Ay me, what act,
That roars so loud and thunders in the index?
Ham. Look here upon this picture and on this, 55
The counterfeit presentment of two brothers.
See what a grace was seated on this brow;
Hyperion's curls; the front of Jove himself;
An eye like Mars, to threaten and command;
A station like the herald Mercury 60
New lighted on a heaven-kissing hill—
A combination and a form indeed

31. **As kill a king:** This is a direct charge of complicity in the murder, but the Queen's replies, and the rest of the play contain no evidence of her guilt.

34. **thy better:** *i.e.* the King.

39. **damned custom:** habitual sinning. **braz'd it so:** made it so brazen.
40. **proof:** *i.e.* like armour of proof. **sense:** feeling.

44. **the rose:** the ornament; the grace.

46. **a blister:** harlots used to be branded on the forehead.

48. **contraction:** *i.e.* the contract of marriage.

50. **rhapsody:** string.
51. **this solidity . . . mass:** *i.e.* the earth.
52. **as against the doom:** as if doomsday were near.

54. **in the index:** in the prologue. The index of a book used to be at the beginning not the end.
56. **counterfeit presentment:** *i.e.* the portrait. Hamlet either points to two portraits hanging on the wall, or, more probably, to two miniatures worn by himself and the Queen.
58. **front:** brow.

60. **station:** posture; bearing.
61. **on a heaven-kissing hill:** This is possibly an echo of Virgil's description of Mercury alighting on Mount Atlas in *Aeneid*, IV.

Where every god did seem to set his seal,
To give the world assurance of a man.
This was your husband. Look you now what follows: 65
Here is your husband, like a mildew'd ear
Blasting his wholesome brother. Have you eyes?
Could you on this fair mountain leave to feed,
And batten on this moor? Ha! have you eyes?
You cannot call it love; for at your age   70
The heyday in the blood is tame, it 's humble,
And waits upon the judgment; and what judgment
Would step from this to this? Sense, sure, you have,
Else could you not have motion; but sure that sense
Is apoplex'd; for madness would not err,   75
Nor sense to ecstasy was ne'er so thrall'd
But it reserv'd some quantity of choice
To serve in such a difference. What devil was 't
That thus hath cozen'd you at hoodman-blind?
Eyes without feeling, feeling without sight,   80
Ears without hands or eyes, smelling sans all,
Or but a sickly part of one true sense
Could not so mope. O shame! where is thy blush?
Rebellious hell,
If thou canst mutine in a matron's bones,   85
To flaming youth let virtue be as wax
And melt in her own fire; proclaim no shame
When the compulsive ardour gives the charge,
Since frost itself as actively doth burn,
And reason panders will.
    Queen.   O Hamlet, speak no more!   90
Thou turn'st my eyes into my very soul;
And there I see such black and grained spots
As will not leave their tinct.
    Ham.   Nay, but to live
In the rank sweat of an enseamed bed,
Stew'd in corruption, honeying and making love   95
Over the nasty sty!
    Queen.   O, speak to me no more!
These words like daggers enter in my ears;

69. **batten:** feed gluttonously on.   **moor:** used with a quibble on Moor, who was dark-skinned and regarded as extremely ugly.   The word thus provides a threefold contrast with *fair mountain.*
71. **heyday:** the high spirits.
72. **waits upon:** follows.
73. **Sense:** feeling.

74. **motion:** impulses; desires.
75. **apoplex'd:** paralysed.
76. **ecstasy:** madness.   **thrall'd:** subservient; enslaved.

78. **To serve in such a difference:** to discriminate between such vast differences.
79. **cozen'd:** cheated; tricked.   **hoodman-blind:** blind-man's buff.

81. **sans:** without.
82. **but a sickly part:** even a diseased fraction.
83. **so mope:** act so foolishly.

87-90. **proclaim no shame . . panders will:** Nothing can be pronounced shameful when it is the result of the compulsive ardour of youth, since now staid middle-age (*frost*) is equally passionate, and uses reason to serve its lust.

92. **grained:** ingrained.
93. **leave their tinct:** give up their colour.
94. **enseamed:** loaded with grease.   This, as Dover Wilson points out, is a technical term from the woollen industry, suggested by *grained* and *tinct,* words associated with wool-dyeing.   As the grease used was hog's lard, this image in its turn suggests the *sty* of line 96.   The language here reveals most clearly how much his mother's marriage has affected him, and his intense disgust, and the dwelling on physical lust suggest some abnormality of mind.

No more, sweet Hamlet.

Ham.   A murderer and a villain!
A slave that is not twentieth part the tithe
Of your precedent lord; a vice of kings;   100
A cutpurse of the empire and the rule,
That from a shelf the precious diadem stole
And put it in his pocket!

Queen.   No more!

Enter GHOST.

Ham.   A king of shreds and patches—
Save me, and hover o'er me with your wings,   105
You heavenly guards! What would your gracious figure?

Queen.   Alas, he 's mad!

Ham.   Do you not come your tardy son to chide,
That laps'd in time and passion, lets go by
Th' important acting of your dread command?   110
O say!

Ghost.   Do not forget; this visitation
Is but to whet thy almost blunted purpose.
But look, amazement on thy mother sits.
O, step between her and her fighting soul!   115
Conceit in weakest bodies strongest works.
Speak to her, Hamlet.

Ham.   How is it with you, lady?

Queen.   Alas, how is 't with you,
That you do bend your eye on vacancy,
And with th' incorporal air do hold discourse?   120
Forth at your eyes your spirits wildly peep;
And, as the sleeping soldiers in th' alarm,
Your bedded hairs like life in excrements
Start up and stand an end. O gentle son,
Upon the heat and flame of thy distemper   125
Sprinkle cool patience! Whereon do you look?

Ham.   On him, on him! Look you how pale he glares.
His form and cause conjoin'd, preaching to stones,
Would make them capable.—Do not look upon me,
Lest with this piteous action you convert   130

100. **precedent lord**: former husband. **a vice of kings**: a clownish villain of a king. In the old Morality Plays, the figure of Vice was usually a mischievous buffoon, who played tricks on the Devil. He was arrayed in fool's dress, the motley "shreds and patches" of line 104.

109. **laps'd in time and passion**: "having let slip both occasion and desire for revenge". An alternative suggested by Dover Wilson is "prisoner of circumstance and passion", since *lapsed* means *arrested* in its only other occurrence in Shakespeare.
110. **important**: urgent.

116. **Conceit**: imagination.

123. **bedded**: lying flat, like "sleeping soldiers". **excrements**: outgrowths; excrescences. The word was used especially of hair, nails, feathers, etc.
126. **Whereon do you look?**: Perhaps the Ghost does not appear to Gertrude in order to spare her suffering, as Bradley suggests. A German play, *Der bestrafte Brudermord*, derived somehow from an English version of *Hamlet*, supplies the explanation that Gertrude is unable to see the Ghost because of her sins.

129. **capable**: *i.e.* of feeling.
130-1. **convert . . . effects**: change my stern purposes.

My stern effects; then what I have to do
Will want true colour—tears perchance for blood.
   Queen. To whom do you speak this?
   Ham.   Do you see nothing there?
   Queen. Nothing at all; yet all that is I see.   134
   Ham. Nor did you nothing hear?
   Queen.   No, nothing but ourselves.
   Ham. Why, look you there.   Look how it steals away.
My father, in his habit as he liv'd!
Look where he goes even now out at the portal.
                              [*Exit* GHOST.
   Queen. This is the very coinage of your brain.
This bodiless creation ecstasy   140
Is very cunning in.
   Ham.   Ecstasy!
My pulse as yours doth temperately keep time,
And makes as healthful music.   It is not madness
That I have utt'red.   Bring me to the test,
And I the matter will re-word which madness   145
Would gambol from.   Mother, for love of grace,
Lay not that flattering unction to your soul,
That not your trespass but my madness speaks:
It will but skin and film the ulcerous place,
Whiles rank corruption, mining all within,   150
Infects unseen.   Confess yourself to heaven;
Repent what 's past; avoid what is to come;
And do not spread the compost on the weeds,
To make them ranker.   Forgive me this my virtue;
For in the fatness of these pursy times   155
Virtue itself of vice must pardon beg,
Yea, curb and woo for leave to do him good.
   Queen. O Hamlet, thou hast cleft my heart in twain.
   Ham. O, throw away the worser part of it,
And live the purer with the other half.   160
Good night—but go not to my uncle's bed;
Assume a virtue, if you have it not.
That monster custom, who all sense doth eat,
Of habits devil, is angel yet in this,

132. want true colour: have the wrong appearance and character. Hamlet quibbles on two meanings of *colour*.

137. in his habit: The Ghost is no longer in armour, but his normal clothes.

140. ecstasy: madness.

145. re-word: repeat in the same words.

147. flattering unction: an oil or salve which promises relief but gives none. Unction is properly an anointment such as *extreme unction* given by a priest to a dying person for spiritual comfort. The application of oil suggests the further image of a medical ointment.

154. this my virtue: my virtuous indignation.
155. pursy: short-winded through being pampered.

157. curb: bow.

163-4. That monster custom . . . in this: Custom, the monster which eats up all natural feeling, and is the devil which controls our habits, is nevertheless in this respect an angel. . . .

That to the use of actions fair and good   165
He likewise gives a frock or livery
That aptly is put on.   Refrain to-night;
And that shall lend a kind of easiness
To the next abstinence; the next more easy;
For use almost can change the stamp of nature,   170
And either curb the devil, or throw him out,
With wondrous potency.   Once more, good night;
And when you are desirous to be blest,
I 'll blessing beg of you.   For this same lord
I do repent; but Heaven hath pleas'd it so,   175
To punish me with this, and this with me,
That I must be their scourge and minister.
I will bestow him, and will answer well
The death I gave him.   So, again, good night.
I must be cruel only to be kind;   180
Thus bad begins and worse remains behind.
One word more, good lady.
    Queen.   What shall I do?
    Ham.   Not this, by no means, that I bid you do:
Let the bloat King tempt you again to bed;
Pinch wanton on your cheek; call you his mouse;   185
And let him, for a pair of reechy kisses,
Or paddling in your neck with his damn'd fingers,
Make you to ravel all this matter out,
That I essentially am not in madness,
But mad in craft.   'Twere good you let him know;   190
For who that 's but a queen, fair, sober, wise,
Would from a paddock, from a bat, a gib,
Such dear concernings hide?   Who would do so?
No, in despite of sense and secrecy,
Unpeg the basket on the house's top,   195
Let the birds fly, and, like the famous ape,
To try conclusions, in the basket creep
And break your own neck down.
    Queen.   Be thou assur'd, if words be made of breath
And breath of life, I have no life to breathe   200
What thou hast said to me.

166. **frock or livery**: suggested by *habits* of line 164.

170. **the stamp of nature**: the natural disposition.

173. **desirous to be blest**: *i.e.* after Gertrude has repented.

177. **their**: *i.e.* of the heavens.
178. **bestow**: pack away; hide.

186. **reechy**: stinking or dirty.

192. **paddock**: a toad. **gib**: a cat.
193. **dear concernings**: concerns touching him so closely.

196. **the famous ape**: an untraced allusion.
197. **To try conclusions**: to test theories; to experiment.

Ham. I must to England; you know that?
Queen.   Alack,
I had forgot. 'Tis so concluded on.
   Ham. There 's letters seal'd; and my two school-fellows,
Whom I will trust as I will adders fang'd—   205
They bear the mandate; they must sweep my way
And marshal me to knavery. Let it work;
For 'tis the sport to have the engineer
Hoist with his own petar; and 't shall go hard
But I will delve one yard below their mines   210
And blow them at the moon. O, 'tis most sweet
When in one line two crafts directly meet.
This man shall set me packing.
I 'll lug the guts into the neighbour room.
Mother, good night. Indeed, this counsellor   215
Is now most still, most secret, and most grave,
Who was in life a foolish prating knave.
Come sir, to draw toward an end with you.
Good night, mother.
        [*Exeunt severally;* HAMLET *tugging in* POLONIUS.

209. **Hoist with his own petar:** blown up by his own explosive. A *petar* was a charge used to blow in a door or breach a wall.

210. **mines:** another military metaphor. Engineers would tunnel under enemy fortifications and then blow them up.

213. **packing:** plotting. The word also plays on the sense of "departing in a hurry".

218. **to draw toward an end:** another pun, on the meanings "close a conversation" and "drag away".

ACT IV

Enter King, Queen, Rosencrantz, *and* Guildenstern.

King. There 's matter in these sighs, these profound
  heaves,
You must translate; 'tis fit we understand them.
Where is your son?
  Queen. Bestow this place on us a little while.
            [*Exeunt* Rosencrantz *and* Guildenstern.
Ah, mine own lord, what have I seen to-night!   5
  King. What, Gertrude? How does Hamlet?
  Queen. Mad as the sea and wind, when both contend
Which is the mightier. In his lawless fit,
Behind the arras hearing something stir,
Whips out his rapier, cries "A rat, a rat!"   10
And in this brainish apprehension kills
The unseen good old man.
  King.   O heavy deed!
It had been so with us had we been there.
His liberty is full of threats to all—
To you yourself, to us, to every one.   15
Alas, how shall this bloody deed be answer'd?
It will be laid to us, whose providence
Should have kept short, restrain'd, and out of haunt,
This mad young man. But so much was our love,
We would not understand what was most fit;   20
But, like the owner of a foul disease,
To keep it from divulging, let it feed
Even on the pith of life. Where is he gone?
  Queen. To draw apart the body he hath kill'd;
O'er whom his very madness, like some ore   25
Among a mineral of metals base,
Shows itself pure: 'a weeps for what is done.

ACT IV. SCENE I

11. **brainish**: rash; headstrong. **apprehension**: notion; fancy.

16. **answer'd**: explained.
17. **providence**: foresight.
18. **kept short**: kept on a short leash or tether. **out of haunt**: away from company.

22. **divulging**: being revealed.

24. **draw apart**: take away.
25. **ore**: *i.e.* gold.
26. **mineral**: mine.

King. O Gertrude, come away!
The sun no sooner shall the mountains touch
But we will ship him hence; and this vile deed   30
We must with all our majesty and skill
Both countenance and excuse. Ho, Guildenstern!

      Re-enter ROSENCRANTZ *and* GUILDENSTERN.

Friends, both go join you with some further aid:
Hamlet in madness hath Polonius slain,
And from his mother's closet he hath dragg'd him;   35
Go seek him out; speak fair, and bring the body
Into the chapel. I pray you haste in this.
          [*Exeunt* ROSENCRANTZ *and* GUILDENSTERN.
Come, Gertrude, we 'll call up our wisest friends
And let them know both what we mean to do
And what 's untimely done; so haply slander—   40
Whose whisper o'er the world's diameter,
As level as the cannon to his blank,
Transports his pois'ned shot—may miss our name,
And hit the woundless air. O, come away!
My soul is full of discord and dismay.   [*Exeunt.*

      SCENE II. *Elsinore. The Castle.*

        Enter HAMLET.

Ham. Safely stow'd.
Gentlemen. [*Within.*] Hamlet! Lord Hamlet!
Ham. But soft! What noise? Who calls on Hamlet? O,
here they come!

      Enter ROSENCRANTZ *and* GUILDENSTERN.

Ros. What have you done, my lord, with the dead body?
Ham. Compounded it with dust, whereto 'tis kin.   6
Ros. Tell us where 'tis, that we may take it thence
And bear it to the chapel.
Ham. Do not believe it.

41. **diameter**: full extent, from one side to the other.
42. **level**: direct. **blank**: the white centre, the bull, of a target.

44. **woundless**: invulncrable.

ACT IV. SCENE II

Ros.   Believe what?   10

Ham.   That I can keep your counsel, and not mine own.
Besides, to be demanded of a sponge—what replication
should be made by the son of a king?

Ros.   Take you me for a sponge, my lord?   14

Ham.   Ay, sir; that soaks up the King's countenance, his
rewards, his authorities. But such officers do the King best
service in the end: he keeps them, like an ape an apple in
the corner of his jaw; first mouth'd to be last swallowed;
when he needs what you have glean'd, it is but squeezing
you and, sponge, you shall be dry again.   20

Ros.   I understand you not, my lord.

Ham.   I am glad of it; a knavish speech sleeps in a foolish
ear.

Ros.   My lord, you must tell us where the body is, and go
with us to the King.   25

Ham.   The body is with the King, but the King is not
with the body. The King is a thing—

Guil.   A thing, my lord!

Ham.   Of nothing. Bring me to him. Hide fox, and all
after.   30

[*Exeunt.*

Scene III.   *Elsinore.   The Castle.*

Enter King, *attended.*

King.   I have sent to seek him, and to find the body.
How dangerous is it that this man goes loose!
Yet must not we put the strong law on him:
He 's lov'd of the distracted multitude,
Who like not in their judgment but their eyes;   5
And where 'tis so, th' offender's scourge is weigh'd,
But never the offence. To bear all smooth and even,
This sudden sending him away must seem
Deliberate pause. Diseases desperate grown
By desperate appliance are reliev'd,   10
Or not at all.

11. **keep your counsel**: keep your secret. Hamlet is perhaps alluding to the fact that he has not betrayed Guildenstern's confession of II. ii. 286.

12. **demanded of**: questioned by. **replication**: reply.

15. **countenance**: favour.

16. **authorities**: offices of authority.

26. **with the King**: deliberate mystification again, possibly meaning "with God, the King of Heaven", or "with the real King, my father". **the King is not with the body** probably refers to Claudius, who will, Hamlet implies, join Polonius later.

27. **thing**: a term of abuse.

29. **Hide fox**: Hamlet darts away, inviting pursuit with this cry, which is possibly from a children's game.

ACT IV. SCENE III

4. **distracted**: *i.e.* easily distracted; fickle.

6. **scourge**: punishment. **weigh'd**: considered.

7. **bear all**: pass everything off.

9. **Deliberate pause**: the result of deliberate reflection.

Enter ROSENCRANTZ.

How now! what hath befall'n?

Ros.   Where the dead body is bestow'd, my lord,
We cannot get from him.

King.   But where is he?

Ros.   Without, my lord; guarded, to know your pleasure.

King.   Bring him before us.   15

Ros.   Ho, Guildenstern! bring in the lord.

Enter HAMLET *and* GUILDENSTERN.

King.   Now, Hamlet, where 's Polonius?

Ham.   At supper.

King.   At supper! Where?   19

Ham.   Not where he eats, but where 'a is eaten; a certain
convocation of politic worms are e'en at him. Your worm is
your only emperor for diet: we fat all creatures else to fat us,
and we fat ourselves for maggots; your fat king and your lean
beggar is but variable service—two dishes, but to one table.
That 's the end.   25

King.   Alas, alas!

Ham.   A man may fish with the worm that hath eat of a
king, and eat of the fish that hath fed of that worm.

King.   What dost thou mean by this?

Ham.   Nothing but to show you how a king may go a
progress through the guts of a beggar.   31

King.   Where is Polonius?

Ham.   In heaven; send thither to see; if your messenger
find him not there, seek him i' th' other place yourself. But
if, indeed, you find him not within this month, you shall nose
him as you go up the stairs into the lobby.   36

King.   [*To* ATTENDANTS.] Go seek him there.

Ham.   'A will stay till you come. [*Exeunt* ATTENDANTS.

King.   Hamlet, this deed, for thine especial safety—
Which we do tender, as we dearly grieve   40
For that which thou hast done—must send thee hence
With fiery quickness. Therefore prepare thyself;
The bark is ready, and the wind at help,
Th' associates tend, and everything is bent

21. **convocation of politic worms:** a jesting reference to the Diet of Worms, and possibly there follows an echo of Montaigne: "The heart and life of a mighty and triumphant emperor is but the breakfast of a seely little worm." The worms are *politic* like the body on whom they feed.

24. **variable service:** different courses.

31. **progress:** the technical term for a royal journey of state.

40. **tender:** care for. Claudius means that he cares for Hamlet's safety as much as he grieves for the death of Polonius.

43. **at help:** favourable.

44. **associates tend:** your companions are waiting.

For England.

Ham.   For England!

King.   Ay, Hamlet.

Ham.   Good!   45

King. So is it, if thou knew'st our purposes.

Ham. I see a cherub that sees them. But, come; for
England! Farewell, dear mother.

King. Thy loving father, Hamlet.   49

Ham. My mother: father and mother is man and wife;
man and wife is one flesh; and so, my mother. Come, for
England.   [*Exit.*

King. Follow him at foot; tempt him with speed aboard;
Delay it not; I 'll have him hence to-night.
Away! for everything is seal'd and done   55
That else leans on th' affair. Pray you make haste.
                         [*Exeunt all but the* KING.
And, England, if my love thou hold'st at aught—
As my great power thereof may give thee sense,
Since yet thy cicatrice looks raw and red
After the Danish sword, and thy free awe   60
Pays homage to us—thou mayst not coldly set
Our sovereign process; which imports at full,
By letters congruing to that effect,
The present death of Hamlet. Do it, England:
For like the hectic in my blood he rages,   65
And thou must cure me. Till I know 'tis done,
Howe'er my haps, my joys were ne'er begun.   [*Exit.*

SCENE IV.   *A plain in Denmark.*

Enter FORTINBRAS *with his* ARMY *over the stage.*

Fort. Go, Captain, from me greet the Danish king.
Tell him that by his licence Fortinbras
Craves the conveyance of a promis'd march
Over his kingdom. You know the rendezvous.
If that his Majesty would aught with us,   5

47. **a cherub:** *i.e.* a guardian angel.

53. **at foot:** at heel; closely.

56. **leans on:** depends on; relates to.

57. **hold'st at aught:** set any value on.

58. **thereof may give thee sense:** may make you aware of it.
59. **cicatrice:** scar.

61. **coldly set:** consider lightly.
62. **sovereign process:** royal decree; order.
63. **congruing:** agreeing.

64. **present:** instant.
65. **hectic:** fever.

67. **Howe'er my haps:** whatever happens to me.

ACT IV. SCENE IV

1. **Go, Captain:** The introduction of Fortinbras at this point does not advance the action, but reminds us of his existence, necessary both for the final scene of the play and as a contrast to Hamlet. William Empson, however, has suggested that the scene is a kind of encore, to be given only when the audience was receiving the play particularly enthusiastically (*Sewanee Review*, Winter and Spring, 1953).

3. **conveyance:** convoy; escort. **promis'd march:** The King had said he would consider the matter only two days previously (*i.e.* on the day before the "mousetrap", and since Hamlet is still in Denmark, it must now be but the day after that event). How has Fortinbras arrived so soon after the ambassadors?

We shall express our duty in his eye;
And let him know so.
 Cap.   I will do 't, my lord.
 Fort. Go softly on.   *[Exeunt all but the* CAPTAIN.

Enter HAMLET, ROSENCRANTZ, GUILDENSTERN, *and* OTHERS.

 Ham. Good sir, whose powers are these?
 Cap. They are of Norway, sir.   10
 Ham. How purpos'd, sir, I pray you?
 Cap. Against some part of Poland.
 Ham. Who commands them, sir?
 Cap. The nephew to old Norway, Fortinbras.
 Ham. Goes it against the main of Poland, sir, 15
Or for some frontier?
 Cap. Truly to speak, and with no addition,
We go to gain a little patch of ground
That hath in it no profit but the name.
To pay five ducats, five, I would not farm it;   20
Nor will it yield to Norway or the Pole
A ranker rate should it be sold in fee.
 Ham. Why, then the Polack never will defend it.
 Cap. Yes, it is already garrison'd.
 Ham. Two thousand souls and twenty thousand ducats 25
Will not debate the question of this straw.
This is th' imposthume of much wealth and peace,
That inward breaks, and shows no cause without
Why the man dies. I humbly thank you, sir.   29
 Cap. God buy you, sir.   *[Exit.*
 Ros.   Will 't please you go, my lord?
 Ham. I 'll be with you straight. Go a little before.
          [Exeunt all but HAMLET.
How all occasions do inform against me,
And spur my dull revenge! What is a man,
If his chief good and market of his time
Be but to sleep and feed? A beast, no more!   35
Sure he that made us with such large discourse,
Looking before and after, gave us not
That capability and godlike reason

6. **his eye:** his presence.

8. **softly:** slowly.

9. **powers:** forces.

15. **the main:** *i.e.* the country as a whole.

18. **a little patch of ground:** G. B. Harrison in *Shakespeare at Work* has pointed out that in 1601-2 Sir Francis Vere heroically defended Ostend from the Spaniards. At one time, Vere had only 1,200 men to oppose a Spanish force 10,000 strong, and one attack resulted in the death of 2,000 men. This scene, therefore, is no doubt another contemporary reference.
20. **To pay:** *i.e.* if I had to pay. **farm:** rent.
22. **ranker:** richer. **in fee:** freehold.

26. **debate:** settle; decide.
27. **imposthume:** an internal abscess or tumour.

32. **all occasions:** *i.e.* the player's speech, the Ghost's reprimand, and now the meeting with Fortinbras.
34. **market of his time:** business of his life.

36. **discourse:** reasoning faculty.

To fust in us unus'd. Now, whether it be
Bestial oblivion, or some craven scruple   40
Of thinking too precisely on th' event—
A thought which, quarter'd, hath but one part wisdom
And ever three parts coward—I do not know
Why yet I live to say "This thing 's to do",
Sith I have cause, and will, and strength, and means,   45
To do 't. Examples gross as earth exhort me:
Witness this army, of such mass and charge,
Led by a delicate and tender prince,
Whose spirit, with divine ambition puff'd,
Makes mouths at the invisible event,   50
Exposing what is mortal and unsure
To all that fortune, death, and danger, dare,
Even for an egg-shell. Rightly to be great
Is not to stir without great argument,
But greatly to find quarrel in a straw,   55
When honour 's at the stake. How stand I, then,
That have a father kill'd, a mother stain'd,
Excitements of my reason and my blood,
And let all sleep, while to my shame I see
The imminent death of twenty thousand men   60
That, for a fantasy and trick of fame,
Go to their graves like beds, fight for a plot
Whereon the numbers cannot try the cause,
Which is not tomb enough and continent
To hide the slain? O, from this time forth,   65
My thoughts be bloody, or be nothing worth!   [*Exit.*

SCENE V. *Elsinore. The Castle.*

Enter QUEEN, HORATIO, *and a* GENTLEMAN.

Queen. I will not speak with her.
Gent. She is importunate, indeed distract.
Her mood will needs be pitied.
Queen.   What would she have?
Gent. She speaks much of her father; says she hears

39. **fust:** moulder.

41. **Of thinking:** *i.e.* which is the result of thinking. **on th' event:** about the (possible) result.

45. **Sith:** since.
46. **gross:** "large" and so, "obvious".

47. **mass and charge:** size and importance.
48. **delicate and tender:** fine and youthful.

50. **Makes mouths . . . event:** makes faces at, mocks at the unforseeable future.
52. **dare:** *i.e.* to inflict.
53. **egg-shell:** Hamlet is critical of Fortinbras's cause, it seems.

54. **argument:** reason; cause.
55. **greatly:** "with all one's might" and "nobly".

58. **blood:** passions.

61. **fantasy and trick:** an illusion and a trifle.

63. **Whereon the numbers . . . cause:** on which the large forces involved cannot decide the question in battle, because it is too small.
64. **continent:** receptacle.

66. **bloody:** *passionate* as well as *murderous*.

ACT IV. SCENE V

There 's tricks i' th' world, and hems, and beats her heart; 5
Spurns enviously at straws; speaks things in doubt,
That carry but half sense. Her speech is nothing,
Yet the unshaped use of it doth move
The hearers to collection; they yawn at it,
And botch the words up fit to their own thoughts;   10
Which, as her winks and nods and gestures yield them,
Indeed would make one think there might be thought,
Though nothing sure, yet much unhappily.
      Hor. 'Twere good she were spoken with; for she may
            strew
Dangerous conjectures in ill-breeding minds.   15
      Queen. Let her come in.   [*Exit* GENTLEMAN.
[*Aside.*] To my sick soul, as sin's true nature is,
Each toy seems prologue to some great amiss.
So full of artless jealousy is guilt,
It spills itself in fearing to be spilt.   20

                  Enter OPHELIA, *distracted.*

      Oph. Where is the beauteous Majesty of Denmark?
      Queen. How now, Ophelia!
      Oph. [*Sings.*]

            How should I your true love know
                  From another one?
            By his cockle hat and staff,   25
                  And his sandal shoon.

      Queen. Alas, sweet lady, what imports this song?
      Oph. Say you? Nay, pray you mark.
[*Sings.*]   He is dead and gone, lady,
                  He is dead and gone;   30
            At his head a grass-green turf,
                  At his heels a stone.
O, ho!
      Queen. Nay, but, Ophelia—
      Oph.   Pray you mark.
[*Sings.*]   White his shroud as the mountain snow—

                  Enter KING.

      Queen. Alas, look here, my lord.   35

6. **Spurns enviously at straws:** kicks spitefully at trifles. Perhaps the expression is metaphorical for "is angry at the slightest cause". **in doubt:** of uncertain meaning.

7. **nothing:** nonsensical; meaningless.

8. **unshaped:** formless; confused. The passage means that though her speech is incoherent, it leads the hearers to infer a meaning.

9. **collection:** deduction; inference. **yawn at it:** gape at it in wonder.

11-13. **Which as her winks . . . unhappily:** the general meaning is that although Ophelia's actions indicate some sort of thought or intention, there is no certainty about it except that she is extremely unhappy.

15. **ill-breeding minds:** minds always thinking evil.

18. **toy:** trifle. **amiss:** disaster; calamity.

19. **artless jealousy:** fears (*i.e.* of detection) lacking in skill and cunning.

20. **spills:** destroys.

21. **Where is the beauteous Majesty of Denmark:** an unconsciously ironical comment on what Gertrude has become. Some of the significance of Ophelia's words in this scene is discussed by W. Empson in *Seven Types of Ambiguity,* pp. 211-14.

25. **cockle hat:** A pilgrim who had crossed the sea wore a cockle shell in his hat. Hamlet, of course, has gone abroad.

Oph.　　　　Larded with sweet flowers;
　　　　　Which bewept to the grave did not go
　　　　　　With true-love showers.

King. How do you, pretty lady?　　　　　　39
Oph. Well, God dild you! They say the owl was a
baker's daughter. Lord, we know what we are, but know
not what we may be. God be at your table!
King. Conceit upon her father.
Oph. Pray let 's have no words of this; but when they ask
you what it means, say you this:　　　　　　45
[*Sings.*]　　　To-morrow is Saint Valentine's day,
　　　　　All in the morning betime,
　　　　　And I a maid at your window,
　　　　　　To be your Valentine.
　　　　　Then up he rose, and donn'd his clothes,　　50
　　　　　　And dupp'd the chamber-door;
　　　　　Let in the maid, that out a maid
　　　　　　Never departed more.

King. Pretty Ophelia!　　　　　　54
Oph. Indeed, la, without an oath, I 'll make an end on 't.
[*Sings.*]　　　By Gis and by Saint Charity,
　　　　　Alack, and fie for shame!
　　　　　Young men will do 't, if they come to 't;
　　　　　　By Cock, they are to blame.
　　　　　Quoth she "Before you tumbled me,　　60
　　　　　　You promis'd me to wed".

He answers:
　　　　　"So would I 'a done, by yonder sun,
　　　　　　An thou hadst not come to my bed".

King. How long hath she been thus?　　　　　　65
Oph. I hope all will be well. We must be patient; but I
cannot choose but weep to think they would lay him i' th'
cold ground. My brother shall know of it; and so I thank
you for your good counsel. Come, my coach! Good night,
ladies; good night, sweet ladies, good night, good night.　70
　　　　　　　　　　　　　　　[*Exit.*
King. Follow her close; give her good watch, I pray you.
　　　　　　　[*Exeunt* HORATIO *and* GENTLEMAN.

36. **Larded**: strewn; adorned.

37. **did not go**: The "not" seems to be an insertion, perhaps because Ophelia refers to the obscure burial of Polonius.

40. **God dild you**: may God reward you. **the owl**: The story alluded to here is a folk tale. Jesus once went into a baker's shop and asked for bread. The mistress put some dough in the oven to bake, but her daughter rebuked her for making the piece too big, and made it smaller. The dough grew miraculously, and the daughter cried, "Heugh, heugh, heugh", in surprise. At this owl-like noise, Jesus turned her into an owl for her lack of charity.

The relevance, of course, is that Ophelia's fortunes have changed as greatly and unexpectedly.

43. **Conceit**: imagining; thinking.

46. **Saint Valentine's day**: the custom was that the first girl seen by a man on St Valentine's morning was his Valentine or true love for the rest of the year. This song reflects Hamlet's treatment of Ophelia—the coarseness of his language to her and his faithlessness (though this last was as much her fault as his).

51. **dupp'd**: opened.

52. **maid**: in the sense of *virgin*.

56. **Gis**: Jesus.

59. **Cock**: God.

O, this is the poison of deep grief; it springs
All from her father's death. And now behold—
O Gertrude, Gertrude!
When sorrows come, they come not single spies,   75
But in battalions! First, her father slain;
Next, your son gone, and he most violent author
Of his own just remove; the people muddied,
Thick and unwholesome in their thoughts and whispers
For good Polonius' death; and we have done but greenly 80
In hugger-mugger to inter him; poor Ophelia
Divided from herself and her fair judgment,
Without the which we are pictures, or mere beasts;
Last, and as much containing as all these,
Her brother is in secret come from France;   85
Feeds on his wonder, keeps himself in clouds,
And wants not buzzers to infect his ear
With pestilent speeches of his father's death;
Wherein necessity, of matter beggar'd,
Will nothing stick our person to arraign   90
In ear and ear. O my dear Gertrude, this,
Like to a murd'ring piece, in many places
Gives me superfluous death.   [*A noise within.*
   Queen.   Alack, what noise is this?
   King. Attend!
              Enter a GENTLEMAN.
Where are my Switzers? Let them guard the door.   95
What is the matter?
   Gent.   Save yourself, my lord:
The ocean, overpeering of his list,
Eats not the flats with more impitious haste
Than young Laertes, in a riotous head,
O'erbears your officers. The rabble call him lord;   100
And, as the world were now but to begin,
Antiquity forgot, custom not known,
The ratifiers and props of every word,
They cry "Choose we; Laertes shall be king".
Caps, hands, and tongues, applaud it to the clouds,   105
"Laertes shall be king, Laertes king".

78. **remove:** removal. **muddied:** unsettled.

80. **greenly:** foolishly; unskilfully.
81. **hugger-mugger:** in secret haste.

84. **as much containing:** with as much importance.

86. **wonder:** grief.
87. **buzzers:** whisperers; spreaders of rumours.

89-91. **Wherein necessity . . . ear:** without real information (*matter*), necessity will drive the rumour-mongers to stick at nothing in accusing the King to everyone.
92. **murd'ring piece:** a cannon loaded with case shot, *i.e.* old nails, scraps of iron, etc., put into a case.

93. **Switzers for his body-guards** The Swiss used to serve all over Europe as mercenaries, and the Pope still has a Swiss guard.

97. **list:** boundary.
98. **flats:** low-lying land near a shore. **impitious:** pitiless; ruthless.
99. **head:** force.

101. **as:** as if.

103. **ratifiers and props:** tradition ratifies and supports every pledge (*word*). The rebels have forgotten the traditional sanctity attached to kingship: *cf.* line 121.

Queen. How cheerfully on the false trail they cry!
                                    [*Noise within.*
O, this is counter, you false Danish dogs!
King. The doors are broke.

Enter LAERTES, *with* OTHERS, *in arms.*

Laer. Where is this king?—Sirs, stand you all without. 110
All. No, let 's come in.
Laer.   I pray you give me leave.
All. We will, we will.   [*Exeunt.*
Laer. I thank you. Keep the door.—O thou vile king,
Give me my father!
  Queen.   Calmly, good Laertes.
  Laer. That drop of blood that 's calm proclaims me
          bastard;   115
Cries cuckold to my father; brands the harlot
Even here, between the chaste unsmirched brow
Of my true mother.
  King.   What is the cause, Laertes,
That thy rebellion looks so giant-like?
Let him go, Gertrude; do not fear our person: 120
There 's such divinity doth hedge a king
That treason can but peep to what it would,
Acts little of his will. Tell me, Laertes,
Why thou art thus incens'd. Let him go, Gertrude.
Speak, man.   125
  Laer. Where is my father?
  King.   Dead.
  Queen.   But not by him.
  King. Let him demand his fill.
  Laer. How came he dead? I 'll not be juggled with.
To hell, allegiance! Vows, to the blackest devil!
Conscience and grace, to the profoundest pit!   130
I dare damnation. To this point I stand,
That both the worlds I give to negligence,
Let come what comes; only I 'll be reveng'd
Most throughly for my father.   134
  King. Who shall stay you?

107. **on the false trail:** The crowd is like a pack of hounds in full cry on a false scent.

108. **counter:** taking up a trail in the wrong direction, *i.e.* away from the quarry.

115. If Laertes is calm, then he is no true son of his father.   Here, if nowhere else, is evidence for delay in Hamlet, for a more vivid example could not be found of "wings as swift as meditation" sweeping to revenge.

116. **brands the harlot:** see note to III. iv. 46.

120. **fear:** fear for.

122-3. **peep to . . . will:** furtively glance at its wishes, and accomplish very little of its desires.

132. **both the worlds:** *i.e.* this and the next.   Laertes is prepared to lose his place in both.

135. **stay:** prevent.

Laer.   My will, not all the world's.
And for my means, I 'll husband them so well
They shall go far with little.
King.   Good Laertes,
If you desire to know the certainty
Of your dear father, is 't writ in your revenge
That, swoopstake, you will draw both friend and foe,   140
Winner and loser?
Laer.   None but his enemies.
King. Will you know them, then?
Laer. To his good friends thus wide I 'll ope my arms
And, like the kind life-rend'ring pelican,
Repast them with my blood.
King.   Why, now you speak   145
Like a good child and a true gentleman.
That I am guiltless of your father's death,
And am most sensibly in grief for it,
It shall as level to your judgment 'pear   149
As day does to your eye.
               [*A noise within:* "Let her come in".
Laer. How now! What noise is that?

Re-enter OPHELIA.

O, heat dry up my brains! tears seven times salt
Burn out the sense and virtue of mine eye!
By heaven, thy madness shall be paid with weight
Till our scale turn the beam. O rose of May!   155
Dear maid, kind sister, sweet Ophelia!
O heavens! is 't possible a young maid's wits
Should be as mortal as an old man's life?
Nature is fine in love; and where 'tis fine
It sends some precious instance of itself   160
After the thing it loves.
Oph. [*Sings.*] They bore him barefac'd on the bier;
          Hey non nonny, nonny, hey nonny;
          And in his grave rain'd many a tear—
Fare you well, my dove!   165

140. **swoopstake:** in a clean sweep, like a gambler winning all stakes at once. **draw:** *i.e.* to destruction.

144. **life-rend'ring pelican:** legend went that the pelican fed its young by piercing its breast and giving them the blood.
145. **Repast:** feed.

148. **sensibly:** feelingly; keenly.
149. **level:** plainly.

153. **virtue!** power

155. **rose of May:** In a phrase, Laertes sums up all the imagery of flowers which has surrounded his sister throughout the play, just as her chatter of flowers which follows symbolises the same association. Her death, too, is "larded with sweet flowers".

159. **Nature:** human nature, and especially the family affections, are implied here.
160. **instance:** token. The token here sent after Polonius is Ophelia's sanity.

Laer. Hadst thou thy wits, and didst persuade revenge,
It could not move thus.

Oph. You must sing "A-down, a-down", and you call him
a-down-a. O, how the wheel becomes it! It is the false
steward, that stole his master's daughter.   170

Laer. This nothing 's more than matter.

Oph. There 's rosemary, that 's for remembrance; pray
you, love, remember. And there is pansies, that 's for
thoughts.

Laer. A document in madness—thoughts and remembrance fitted.   176

Oph. There 's fennel for you, and columbines. There 's
rue for you; and here 's some for me. We may call it herb
of grace a Sundays. O, you must wear your rue with a
difference. There 's a daisy. I would give you some violets,
but they wither'd all when my father died. They say 'a made
a good end.   182

[*Sings*.]   For bonny sweet Robin is all my joy.

Laer. Thought and affliction, passion, hell itself,
She turns to favour and to prettiness.   185

Oph. [*Sings*.] And will 'a not come again?
          And will 'a not come again?
              No, no, he is dead,
              Go to thy death-bed,
          He never will come again.   190

          His beard was as white as snow,
          All flaxen was his poll;
              He is gone, he is gone,
              And we cast away moan:
          God-a-mercy on his soul!   195

And of all Christian souls, I pray God. God buy you. [*Exit*.

Laer. Do you see this, O God?

King. Laertes, I must commune with your grief,
Or you deny me right. Go but apart,
Make choice of whom your wisest friends you will,   200
And they shall hear and judge 'twixt you and me.
If by direct or by collateral hand

168. **and**: if.

169. **the wheel**: most easily explained as "refrain; chorus", with a quibble on the wheel of fortune (see II. ii. 477) which has brought Polonius "down".

169-70. **false steward**: an untraced allusion.

171. **This nothing . . . matter**: this nonsense conveys more meaning than any sense.

172. **rosemary**: Ophelia is using the language of flowers, in which rosemary symbolises remembrance. Laertes has to remember, just as the Ghost warned Hamlet, "Remember me".

175. **document**: precept; lesson.

177. **fennel**: symbol of flattery and deceit, and **columbine**, faithlessness in marriage, are given to Claudius.

178. **rue**: emblem of repentance and sorrow, for the Queen and herself respectively.

179-80. **with a difference**: an heraldic term, but here no doubt implying that the queen wears rue for repentance, while she has it for grief. **daisy**: for deceit, given perhaps to the queen, or the king. **violets**: representing faithfulness.

183. **bonny sweet Robin**: a popular ballad in Shakespeare's day, of which the words are lost.

184. **Thought**: melancholy. **passion**: suffering.

185. **favour**: charm.

196. **of**: on.

200. **of whom . . . you will**: whichever of your wisest friends you wish.

They find us touch'd, we will our kingdom give,
Our crown, our life, and all that we call ours,
To you in satisfaction; but if not,   205
Be you content to lend your patience to us,
And we shall jointly labour with your soul
To give it due content.
    Laer.   Let this be so.
His means of death, his obscure funeral—
No trophy, sword, nor hatchment, o'er his bones,   210
No noble rite nor formal ostentation—
Cry to be heard, as 'twere from heaven to earth,
That I must call 't in question.
    King.   So you shall;
And where th' offence is, let the great axe fall.
I pray you go with me.   *[Exeunt.*

SCENE VI. *Elsinore. The Castle.*

Enter HORATIO *with an* ATTENDANT.

    Hor. What are they that would speak with me?
    Att. Sea-faring men, sir; they say they have letters for you.
    Hor. Let them come in.   *[Exit* ATTENDANT.
I do not know from what part of the world
I should be greeted, if not from Lord Hamlet.   5

Enter SAILORS.

    Sail. God bless you, sir.
    Hor. Let Him bless thee too.   7
    Sail. 'A shall, sir, an 't please Him. There 's a letter for
you, sir; it came from th' ambassador that was bound for
England—if your name be Horatio, as I am let to know
it is.   11
    Hor. *[Reads.]* "Horatio, when thou shalt have over-
look'd this, give these fellows some means to the King: they
have letters for him. Ere we were two days old at sea, a
pirate of very warlike appointment gave us chase. Finding
ourselves too slow of sail, we put on a compelled valour; and

203. **touch'd**: implicated.

210. **trophy, sword, nor hatchment**: over the tomb of a knight were hung his arms, armour, and escutcheon. **hatchment**: escutcheon.
211. **ostentation**: pomp.

ACT IV.   SCENE VI

12. **overlook'd**: perused; read.
13. **means to**: means of access to.

15. **appointment**: equipment.

in the grapple I boarded them. On the instant they got clear
of our ship; so I alone became their prisoner. They have
dealt with me like thieves of mercy; but they knew what
they did; I am to do a good turn for them. Let the King
have the letters I have sent; and repair thou to me with as
much speed as thou wouldest fly death. I have words to
speak in thine ear will make thee dumb; yet are they much
too light for the bore of the matter. These good fellows will
bring thee where I am. Rosencrantz and Guildenstern hold
their course for England; of them I have much to tell thee.
Farewell.

              He that thou knowest thine, HAMLET."   28
Come, I will give you way for these your letters,
And do 't the speedier that you may direct me   30
To him from whom you brought them.   [*Exeunt*.

       SCENE VII. *Elsinore. The Castle.*

         Enter KING *and* LAERTES.

  King. Now must your conscience my acquittance seal,
And you must put me in your heart for friend,
Sith you have heard, and with a knowing ear,
That he which hath your noble father slain
Pursu'd my life.
    Laer.   It well appears. But tell me   5
Why you proceeded not against these feats,
So crimeful and so capital in nature,
As by your safety, wisdom, all things else, '
You mainly were stirr'd up.
    King.   O, for two special reasons,
Which may to you, perhaps, seem much unsinew'd,   10
But yet to me th' are strong. The Queen his mother
Lives almost by his looks; and for myself,
My virtue or my plague, be it either which—
She is so conjunctive to my life and soul
That, as the star moves not but in his sphere,   15
I could not but by her. The other motive,

19. **thieves of mercy**: *i.e.* merciful thieves.

24. **bore**: calibre. Hamlet's words are not big enough for the news he has to tell, as a small shot is unsuitable for a gun of large calibre.

ACT IV. SCENE VII

1. **Now must your conscience**: This conversation is continued from Scene iii, the part we miss being what we know already of Polonius's death. **acquittance**: discharge, *i.e.* from guilt.
3. **Sith**: since. **knowing**: understanding.

5. **Pursu'd**: sought to take.
6. **feats**: deeds.

9. **mainly**: strongly.
10. **unsinew'd**: without sinews, *i.e.* weak.

13. **My virtue . . . which**: whether it be a fine quality or a fault in me.
14. **conjunctive**: closely united to.
15. **as the star**: the image is suggested by *conjunctive*, an astrological term. Each planet (*star*) was thought to be fixed to a hollow, transparent sphere, whose rotation caused the movement of the planet round the earth.

Why to a public count I might not go,
Is the great love the general gender bear him;
Who, dipping all his faults in their affection,
Work like the spring that turneth wood to stone,   20
Convert his gyves to graces; so that my arrows,
Too slightly timber'd for so loud a wind,
Would have reverted to my bow again,
But not where I had aim'd them.
     Laer. And so have I a noble father lost;   25
A sister driven into desp'rate terms,
Whose worth, if praises may go back again,
Stood challenger on mount of all the age
For her perfections.   But my revenge will come.
     King. Break not your sleeps for that. You must not think
That we are made of stuff so flat and dull   31
That we can let our beard be shook with danger,
And think it pastime.   You shortly shall hear more.
I lov'd your father, and we love our self;
And that, I hope, will teach you to imagine—   35

                Enter a MESSENGER *with letters.*

How now! What news?
     Mess.   Letters, my lord, from Hamlet:
These to your Majesty; this to the Queen.
     King. From Hamlet! Who brought them?
     Mess. Sailors, my lord, they say; I saw them not.
They were given me by Claudio; he receiv'd them   40
Of him that brought them.
     King.   Laertes, you shall hear them.
Leave us.   [*Exit* MESSENGER.
     [*Reads.*] "High and Mighty. You shall know I am set
naked on your kingdom. To-morrow shall I beg leave to see
your kingly eyes; when I shall, first asking your pardon there-
unto, recount the occasion of my sudden and more strange
return.   47
                                        HAMLET."
What should this mean?   Are all the rest come back?
Or is it some abuse, and no such thing?   '   50

17. **count:** reckoning, *i.e.* trial.
18. **general gender:** common people.

20. **like the spring:** the image is of water capable of petrifying wood.
21. **gyves:** fetters.
22. **Too slightly timber'd:** of too light a wood.

26. **terms:** condition.
27. **go back again:** be applied to what existed only in the past.
28. **challenger on mount:** on high as a challenger.

33. **You shortly shall hear more:** Why does Claudius take so long to tell Laertes that he has already sent Hamlet to his death? Note that he is equally circumspect about his proposal for the fencing match (lines 107-40).

43. **naked:** destitute.

50. **abuse:** trick; deception.

Laer. Know you the hand?

King. 'Tis Hamlet's character. "Naked"!
And in a postscript here, he says "alone".
Can you advise me?

    Laer. I am lost in it, my lord. But let him come;   55
It warms the very sickness in my heart
That I shall live and tell him to his teeth
"Thus didest thou".

    King.   If it be so, Laertes—
As how should it be so, how otherwise?—
Will you be rul'd by me?

    Laer.   Ay, my lord;   60
So you will not o'errule me to a peace.

    King. To thine own peace. If he be now return'd,
As checking at his voyage, and that he means
No more to undertake it, I will work him
To an exploit now ripe in my device,   65
Under the which he shall not choose but fall;
And for his death, no wind of blame shall breathe;
But even his mother shall uncharge the practice
And call it accident.

    Laer.   My lord, I will be rul'd
The rather, if you could devise it so   70
That I might be the organ.

    King.   It falls right.
You have been talk'd of since your travel much,
And that in Hamlet's hearing, for a quality
Wherein they say you shine. Your sum of parts
Did not together pluck such envy from him   75
As did that one; and that, in my regard,
Of the unworthiest siege.

    Laer.   What part is that, my lord?

    King. A very riband in the cap of youth,
Yet needful too; for youth no less becomes
The light and careless livery that it wears   80
Than settled age his sables and his weeds,
Importing health and graveness. Two months since
Here was a gentleman of Normandy—

52. **character:** handwriting.

55. **lost:** perplexed.

59. **how should it:** We expect "How should it *not*" but perhaps the King for a moment reveals incredulity, and then, with "how otherwise", accepts the evidence of the handwriting's being Hamlet's.

63. **checking at:** "abandoning", like a falcon forsaking its proper game to follow another.

68. **uncharge the practice:** never suspect the plot.

71. **organ:** instrument.

74. **Your sum of parts:** all your accomplishments.

77. **unworthiest siege:** lowest rank; least importance.

80. **livery:** dress.
81. **sables:** furred clothes. **weeds:** dress.
82. **health:** prosperity.

I have seen myself, and serv'd against, the French,
And they can well on horseback; but this gallant   85
Had witchcraft in 't; he grew into his seat,
And to such wondrous doing brought his horse,
As had he been incorps'd and demi-natur'd
With the brave beast. So far he topp'd my thought,
That I, in forgery of shapes and tricks,   90
Come short of what he did.
    Laer.   A Norman was 't?
    King. A Norman.
    Laer. Upon my life, Lamord.
    King.   The very same.
    Laer. I know him well. He is the brooch indeed
And gem of all the nation.   95
    King. He made confession of you;
And gave you such a masterly report
For art and exercise in your defence,
And for your rapier most especial,
That he cried out 'twould be a sight indeed   100
If one could match you. The scrimers of their nation
He swore had neither motion, guard, nor eye,
If you oppos'd them. Sir, this report of his
Did Hamlet so envenom with his envy
That he could nothing do but wish and beg   105
Your sudden coming o'er, to play with you.
Now out of this—
    Laer.   What out of this, my lord?
    King. Laertes, was your father dear to you?
Or are you like the painting of a sorrow,
A face without a heart?
    Laer.   Why ask you this?   110
    King. Not that I think you did not love your father;
But that I know love is begun by time,
And that I see, in passages of proof,
Time qualifies the spark and fire of it.
There lives within the very flame of love   115
A kind of wick or snuff that will abate it;
And nothing is at a like goodness still;

85. **can well:** are skilful.

88. **incorps'd:** *i.e.* as if he had been made into one body with.

90. **in forgery:** in devising.   The rider performed tricks which Claudius was incapable even of imagining.

93. **Lamord:** Some personal reference seems to be intended, with the elaborate description of his horsemanship, but the subject has not been traced.
94. **brooch:** ornament.

96. **made confession:** *i.e.* admitted Laertes's superiority.
97. **masterly report:** reporting him to be a master.
98. **defence:** fencing.

101. **scrimers:** fencers.
102. **motion:** attack.

112. **by time:** *i.e.* by occasions, or circumstances.
113. **passages of proof:** incidents that have been verified.

115-16. Are we to take from these lines a hint that Gertrude's conscience was pricked by Hamlet's exhortations in III. iv?
117. **at a like goodness still:** always in the same state of excellence.

For goodness, growing to a pleurisy,
Dies in his own too much. That we would do,
We should do when we would; for this "would" changes, 120
And hath abatements and delays as many
As there are tongues, are hands, are accidents;
And then this "should" is like a spendthrift's sigh
That hurts by easing. But to the quick of th' ulcer:
Hamlet comes back; what would you undertake   125
To show yourself in deed your father's son
More than in words?
  Laer.   To cut his throat i' th' church.
  King. No place, indeed, should murder sanctuarize;
Revenge should have no bounds. But, good Laertes,
Will you do this? Keep close within your chamber.   130
Hamlet return'd shall know you are come home.
We 'll put on those shall praise your excellence,
And set a double varnish on the fame
The Frenchman gave you; bring you, in fine, together,
And wager on your heads. He, being remiss,   135
Most generous, and free from all contriving,
Will not peruse the foils; so that with ease
Or with a little shuffling, you may choose
A sword unbated, and, in a pass of practice,
Requite him for your father.
  Laer.   I will do 't;   140
And for that purpose I 'll anoint my sword.
I bought an unction of a mountebank,
So mortal that but dip a knife in it,
Where it draws blood no cataplasm so rare,
Collected from all simples that have virtue   145
Under the moon, can save the thing from death
That is but scratch'd withal. I 'll touch my point
With this contagion, that, if I gall him slightly,
It may be death.
  King.   Let 's further think of this;
Weigh what convenience both of time and means   150
May fit us to our shape. If this should fail,
And that our drift look through our bad performance,

118. **pleurisy**: surfeit.
119-24. **That we would . . . easing**: what we desire to do, we should do at once, for the desire is subject to diminution or delay through the words (**tongues**) and actions (**hands**) of others, or through accidents; afterwards, though the thought of what we could have done is a comfort, we have really done ourselves harm. **spendthrift's sigh**: sighs were believed to cause loss of blood, so a spendthrift sighing for his lost wealth might ease his sorrow, but harm his body. (cp. *2 Henry VI*, III. ii., "blood-drinking sighs".)

127. **i' th' church**: A contrast with the Hamlet of III. iii.
128. **sanctuarize**: provide sanctuary for.

132. **put on those shall praise**: set people to praise

134. **in fine**: in the end.
135. **remiss**: careless; off his guard.

137. **peruse**: examine carefully.

139. **unbated**: unblunted. **pass of practice**: a *practice bout*, with an ironic pun on a *treacherous thrust*.

141. **I 'll anoint my sword**: Claudius need not have been so careful in his approach to Laertes: the young man is as treacherous as the King
142. **unction**: ointment. **mountebank**: quack doctor.
143. **mortal**: deadly.
144. **cataplasm**: plaster.
145. **simples**: *ingredients* (in a medicine), and hence *herbs*. **virtue**: power (*i.e.* to heal).
146. **Under the moon**: see note on III. ii. 245.

148. **contagion**: poison.

151. **fit us to our shape**: be suitable for our plan.
152. **our drift . . . performance**: our intention is revealed by our incompetence.

'Twere better not assay'd, therefore this project
Should have a back or second, that might hold
If this did blast in proof. Soft! let me see.   155
We 'll make a solemn wager on your cunnings—
I ha 't.
When in your motion you are hot and dry—
As make your bouts more violent to that end—
And that he calls for drink, I 'll have preferr'd him   160
A chalice for the nonce; whereon but sipping,
If he by chance escape your venom'd stuck,
Our purpose may hold there. But stay; what noise?

Enter QUEEN.

   Queen. One woe doth tread upon another's heel,
So fast they follow. Your sister 's drown'd, Laertes.   165
   Laer. Drown'd? O, where?
   Queen. There is a willow grows aslant the brook
That shows his hoar leaves in the glassy stream;
Therewith fantastic garlands did she make
Of crowflowers, nettles, daisies, and long purples   170
That liberal shepherds give a grosser name,
But our cold maids do dead men's fingers call them.
There, on the pendent boughs her coronet weeds
Clamb'ring to hang, an envious sliver broke;
When down her weedy trophies and herself   175
Fell in the weeping brook. Her clothes spread wide
And, mermaid-like, awhile they bore her up;
Which time she chanted snatches of old lauds,
As one incapable of her own distress,
Or like a creature native and indued   180
Unto that element; but long it could not be
Till that her garments, heavy with their drink,
Pull'd the poor wretch from her melodious lay
To muddy death.
   Laer.   Alas, then she is drown'd!
   Queen. Drown'd, drown'd.   185
   Laer. Too much of water hast thou, poor Ophelia,
And therefore I forbid my tears; but yet

155. **blast in proof:** explode when being tried, like a cannon under test.
156. **your cunnings:** your respective skills.

160. **preferr'd:** offered.
161. **the nonce:** the occasion.
162. **stuck:** thrust.

167. **willow:** emblem of forsaken love.

170. **crowflowers:** buttercups, or perhaps crowfoot. **long purples:** the purple orchis.
171. **liberal:** *free-spoken*, or perhaps *licentious*. **a grosser name:** one of these was *rampant widow* which the Queen might well wish to avoid.

174. **sliver:** branch.

178. **lauds:** psalms; songs.
179. **incapable:** *i.e.* of realising.
180. **indued:** endowed (with the qualities which fitted her to live in water).

It is our trick; nature her custom holds,
Let shame say what it will. When these are gone,
The woman will be out. Adieu, my lord. 190
I have a speech o' fire that fain would blaze
But that this folly douts it.   [*Exit.*
   King.   Let 's follow, Gertrude.
How much I had to do to calm his rage!
Now fear I this will give it start again;
Therefore let 's follow.   [*Exeunt.*

188. **trick:** habit.

190. **The woman will be out:** his unmanliness will be purged when he has shed his tears.

192. **this folly:** *i.e.* his weeping. **douts:** extinguishes.

ACT V

Scene I. *Elsinore. A churchyard.*

Enter two Clowns *with spades and picks.*

First Clo. Is she to be buried in Christian burial when she wilfully seeks her own salvation?

Sec. Clo. I tell thee she is; therefore make her grave straight. The crowner hath sat on her, and finds it Christian burial.   5

First Clo. How can that be, unless she drown'd herself in her own defence?

Sec. Clo. Why, 'tis found so.

First Clo. It must be "se offendendo"; it cannot be else. For here lies the point: if I drown myself wittingly, it argues an act; and an act hath three branches—it is to act, to do, to perform; argal, she drown'd herself wittingly.   12

Sec. Clo. Nay, but hear you, Goodman Delver.

First Clo. Give me leave. Here lies the water; good. Here stands the man; good. If the man go to this water and drown himself, it is, will he, nill he, he goes—mark you that; but if the water come to him and drown him, he drowns not himself. Argal, he that is not guilty of his own death shortens not his own life.

Sec. Clo. But is this law?   20

First Clo. Ay, marry, is 't; crowner's quest law.

Sec. Clo. Will you ha' the truth an 't? If this had not been a gentlewoman, she should have been buried out a Christian burial.   24

First Clo. Why, there thou say'st; and the more pity that great folk should have count'nance in this world to drown or hang themselves more than their even Christen. Come, my spade. There is no ancient gentlemen but gard'ners, ditchers, and grave-makers; they hold up Adam's profession.   30

Sec. Clo. Was he a gentleman?

First Clo. 'A was the first that ever bore arms.

216

ACT V. SCENE I

2. **salvation:** a malapropism; cp. *Much Ado*, III. iii. 2. "It were pity but they should suffer salvation body and soul."

4. **straight:** straightway; immediately. **crowner:** coroner. **finds it:** gives a verdict for.

9. **se offendendo:** a malapropism for *se defendendo* (self defence).

12. **argal:** a corruption of *ergo*, Latin for *therefore*, used in learned argument.

21. **quest:** inquest. The whole of this dialogue is probably ridiculing a famous case, arising from the suicide by drowning of Sir James Hales, in which arguments similar to and as comical as the clown's were used. They included the division of an act into three parts, and the question of whether Hales *committed* the drowning or *suffered* it.

22. **ha':** have. **an 't:** of it. Shakespeare is reproducing colloquial common speech.

25. **thou say'st:** you are right; cp. the modern idiom, "You've said it".

26. **have count'nance:** cp. our "have the face to".

27. **even Christen:** fellow Christian.

32. **bore arms:** punning on the meaning of *arms* as *escutcheon*.

Sec. Clo. Why, he had none.

First Clo. What, art a heathen? How dost thou understand the Scripture? The Scripture says Adam digg'd. Could he dig without arms? I 'll put another question to thee. If thou answerest me not to the purpose, confess thyself—

Sec. Clo. Go to.   39

First Clo. What is he that builds stronger than either the mason, the shipwright, or the carpenter?

Sec. Clo. The gallows-maker; for that frame outlives a thousand tenants.   43

First Clo. I like thy wit well; in good faith the gallows does well; but how does it well? It does well to those that do ill. Now thou dost ill to say the gallows is built stronger than the church; argal, the gallows may do well to thee. To 't again, come.

Sec. Clo. Who builds stronger than a mason, a shipwright, or a carpenter?   50

First Clo. Ay, tell me that, and unyoke.

Sec. Clo. Marry, now I can tell.

First Clo. To 't.

Sec. Clo. Mass, I cannot tell.   54

Enter HAMLET *and* HORATIO, *afar off.*

First Clo. Cudgel thy brains no more about it, for your dull ass will not mend his pace with beating; and when you are ask'd this question next, say "a grave-maker": the houses he makes lasts till doomsday. Go, get thee to Yaughan; fetch me a stoup of liquor. [*Exit* SECOND CLOWN. [*Digs and sings.*] In youth, when I did love, did love,   60
        Methought it was very sweet,
     To contract-o-the time for-a my behove,
        O, methought there-a-was nothing-a meet.

Ham. Has this fellow no feeling of his business, that 'a sings in grave-making?   65

Hor. Custom hath made it in him a property of easiness.

Ham. 'Tis e'en so; the hand of little employment hath the daintier sense.

37. **to the purpose:** correctly. **confess thyself:** a proverbial saying, which ends "and be hanged".

51. **unyoke:** be done with it (as one is done with a horse after ploughing).

59. **Yaughan:** perhaps a topical allusion, the name may be a corruption of John or Johan. **stoup:** flagon.

60. **In youth,** etc.: this song is a somewhat garbled version of *The Aged Lover Renounceth Love*, from *Tottel's Miscellany* (1557), and attributed to Lord Vaux. The relevant stanzas are—

> "I lothe that I did loue,
> In youth that I thought sweet
> As time requires for my behoue
> Me thinkes they are not mete.
>
> For age with steylying steppes,
> Hath clawed me with his cowche (crowch),
> And lusty life away she leapes,
> As there had bene none such.
>
> A pikeax and a spade
> And eke a shrowdyng shete,
> A house of claye for to be made,
> For such a gest most mete."

The *o* and *a* are the grunts of the Clown as he digs.

66. **a property of easiness:** a thing that is easy for him, or to which he is indifferent.

First Clo. [*Sings.*] But age, with his stealing steps,
      Hath clawed me in his clutch,   70
And hath shipped me intil the land,
      As if I had never been such.

                     [*Throws up a skull.*

Ham. That skull had a tongue in it, and could sing once.
How the knave jowls it to the ground, as if 'twere Cain's
jawbone, that did the first murder! This might be the pate
of a politician, which this ass now o'erreaches; one that
would circumvent God, might it not?

Hor. It might, my lord.   78

Ham. Or of a courtier; which could say "Good morrow,
sweet lord! How dost thou, sweet lord?" This might be
my Lord Such-a-one, that praised my Lord Such-a-one's
horse, when 'a meant to beg it—might it not?

Hor. Ay, my lord.   83

Ham. Why, e'en so; and now my Lady Worm's, chapless,
and knock'd about the mazard with a sexton's spade. Here's
fine revolution, and we had the trick to see 't. Did these
bones cost no more the breeding but to play at loggats with
them? Mine ache to think on 't.

First Clo. [*Sings.*] A pick-axe and a spade, a spade,
      For and a shrouding sheet: 90
O, a pit of clay for to be made
      For such a guest is meet.

                   [*Throws up another skull.*

Ham. There's another. Why may not that be the skull
of a lawyer? Where be his quiddities now, his quillets, his
cases, his tenures, and his tricks? Why does he suffer this
rude knave now to knock him about the sconce with a dirty
shovel, and will not tell him of his action of battery? Hum!
This fellow might be in 's time a great buyer of land, with
his statutes, his recognizances, his fines, his double vouchers,
his recoveries. Is this the fine of his fines, and the recovery
of his recoveries, to have his fine pate full of fine dirt? Will
his vouchers vouch him no more of his purchases, and
double ones too, than the length and breadth of a pair of
indentures? The very conveyances of his lands will scarcely

71. **intil:** into.

74. **jowls:** knocks. **Cain's jawbone:** Cain was said to have killed Abel with the jawbone of an ass.
76. **politician:** schemer; intriguer. **o'erreaches:** there is a pun on the meaning "gets the better of".

84. **chapless:** without the under-jaw.
85. **mazard:** slang word for "head".
86. **fine revolution:** wonderful change. **and:** if. **trick:** skill; knack.
87. **loggats:** a game similar to bowls, played with small logs (loggats) about 2¼ inches long.

94. **quiddities . . . quillets:** legal subtleties and quibbles.

96. **sconce:** head.

99. **statutes:** bonds. **recognizances:** another form of bonds. **fines . . . recoveries:** allusions to a process of *fine and recovery*, in which an entail might be formally barred, and which could be *vouched* for by two people **(double vouchers)** who would warrant the party's title.
100. **fine of his fines:** the end of his fines. In this passage, *fine* is used in four senses: **(1)** end; **(2)** as a legal term; **(3)** clever, capable; **(4)** small. **recovery of:** return for.
104. **indentures:** these were duplicates, written on one sheet, of an agreement. The two were cut apart along an *indented* line, so that each might be proved genuine by fitting it to the other.

lie in this box; and must th' inheritor himself have no more, ha?

Hor.   Not a jot more, my lord.   106

Ham.   Is not parchment made of sheep-skins?

Hor.   Ay, my lord, and of calves' skins too.

Ham.   They are sheep and calves which seek out assurance in that. I will speak to this fellow. Whose grave 's this, sirrah?

First Clo.   Mine, sir.

[*Sings.*]   O, a pit of clay for to be made

                         For such a guest is meet.   115

Ham.   I think it be thine, indeed, for thou liest in 't.

First Clo.   You lie out on 't, sir, and therefore 'tis not yours. For my part, I do not lie in 't, yet it is mine.

Ham.   Thou dost lie in 't, to be in 't and say it is thine; 'tis for the dead, not for the quick; therefore thou liest.   120

First Clo.   'Tis a quick lie, sir; 'twill away again from me to you.

Ham.   What man dost thou dig it for?

First Clo.   For no man, sir.

Ham.   What woman, then?   125

First Clo.   For none neither.

Ham.   Who is to be buried in 't?

First Clo.   One that was a woman, sir; but, rest her soul, she 's dead.   129

Ham.   How absolute the knave is! We must speak by the card, or equivocation will undo us. By the Lord, Horatio, this three years I have took note of it: the age is grown so picked that the toe of the peasant comes so near the heel of the courtier, he galls his kibe. How long hast thou been a grave-maker?   135

First Clo   Of all the days i' th' year, I came to 't that day that our last King Hamlet overcame Fortinbras.

Ham.   How long is that since?

First Clo.   Cannot you tell that? Every fool can tell that: it was that very day that young Hamlet was born—he that is mad, and sent into England.   141

Ham.   Ay, marry, why was he sent into England?

105. **box**: the skull, as Dover Wilson points out, which, with its "parchment-like surface and serrated sutures" suggests the *indentures* of line 104. It cannot refer to the grave or coffin which would surely hold a large number of conveyances. **inheritor**: owner.

110. **assurance**: another pun, on (1) security, (2) conveyance of land.
111. **that**: *i.e.* parchment.

116. **liest**: *tell lies,* and also *are placed.* The dialogue which follows depends on the double meaning.

120. **quick**: living.

130. **absolute**: *positive,* and also *complete* (*i.e.* completely knavish).
130-1. by the card: precisely. The image is of a compass card, or a map.
131. **equivocation**: ambiguity.

133. **picked**: refined; fastidious.
134. **kibe**: chilblain.

First Clo. Why, because 'a was mad; 'a shall recover his wits there; or, if 'a do not, 'tis no great matter there.

Ham. Why?   145

First Clo. 'Twill not be seen in him there: there the men are as mad as he.

Ham. How came he mad?

First Clo. Very strangely, they say.

Ham. How strangely?   150

First Clo. Faith, e'en with losing his wits.

Ham. Upon what ground?

First Clo. Why, here in Denmark. I have been sexton here, man and boy, thirty years.

Ham. How long will a man lie i' th' earth ere he rot? 155

First Clo. Faith, if 'a be not rotten before 'a die—as we have many pocky corses now-a-days that will scarce hold the laying in—'a will last you some eight year or nine year. A tanner will last you nine year.

Ham. Why he more than another?   160

First Clo. Why, sir, his hide is so tann'd with his trade that 'a will keep out water a great while; and your water is a sore decayer of your whoreson dead body. Here 's a skull now; this skull has lien you i' th' earth three and twenty years.   165

Ham. Whose was it?

First Clo. A whoreson mad fellow's it was. Whose do you think it was?

Ham. Nay, I know not.   169

First Clo. A pestilence on him for a mad rogue! 'A poured a flagon of Rhenish on my head once. This same skull, sir, was, sir, Yorick's skull, the King's jester.

Ham. This?

First Clo. E'en that.   174

Ham. Let me see. [*Takes the skull.*] Alas, poor Yorick! I knew him, Horatio: a fellow of infinite jest, of most excellent fancy; he hath borne me on his back a thousand times. And now how abhorred in my imagination it is! My gorge rises at it. Here hung those lips that I have kiss'd I know not how oft. Where be your gibes now, your gambols, your

152. **Upon what ground:** Hamlet means, "For what reason?"

154. **thirty years:** This, with the reference to Yorick's death (lines 164-5) fixes Hamlet's age. The play, however, makes Hamlet appear much less mature than this, especially in the first half.

157. **pocky:** pock-marked.

164. **lien:** lain.

178-9. **My gorge rises:** my stomach turns. **gorge:** means *throat*, literally.

songs, your flashes of merriment that were wont to set the
table on a roar?   Not one now to mock your own grinning
—quite chap-fall'n?   Now get you to my lady's chamber,
and tell her, let her paint an inch thick, to this favour she
must come; make her laugh at that.   Prithee, Horatio, tell
me one thing.   186

   Hor.   What 's that, my lord?

   Ham.   Dost thou think Alexander look'd a this fashion i'
th' earth?

   Hor.   E'en so.   190

   Ham.   And smelt so? Pah!   [*Throws down the skull.*

   Hor.   E'en so, my lord.

   Ham.   To what base uses we may return, Horatio!   Why
may not imagination trace the noble dust of Alexander till
'a find it stopping a bung-hole?   195

   Hor.   'Twere to consider too curiously to consider so.

   Ham.   No, faith, not a jot; but to follow him thither with
modesty enough, and likelihood to lead it, as thus: Alexander died, Alexander was buried, Alexander returneth to
dust; the dust is earth; of earth we make loam; and why of
that loam whereto he was converted might they not stop a
beer-barrel?   202

      Imperious Caesar, dead and turn'd to clay,
      Might stop a hole to keep the wind away.

      O, that that earth which kept the world in awe   205
      Should patch a wall t' expel the winter's flaw!
But soft! but soft! awhile.   Here comes the King.

Enter the KING, QUEEN, LAERTES, *in funeral procession after
   the coffin, with* PRIEST *and* LORDS *attendant.*

The Queen, the courtiers.   Who is this they follow?
And with such maimed rites?   This doth betoken
The corse they follow did with desperate hand   210
Fordo it own life.   'Twas of some estate.
Couch we awhile and mark.   [*Retiring with* HORATIO.

   Laer.   What ceremony else?

   Ham.   That is Laertes, a very noble youth. Mark.

   Laer.   What ceremony else?   215

183. **chap-fall'n**: *dejected* and also *without a lower jaw*.
184. **favour**: appearance.

196. **curiously**: fancifully; particularly.

197-8. **with modesty enough, and likelihood to lead it**: following the most moderate and likely course of argument.

201. **loam**: plasterer's mixture of water, clay, straw, horse-dung, etc.
203. **Imperious**: imperial.

206. **flaw**: gust of wind.

209. **maimed**: imperfect.

211. **Fordo**: destroy. **estate**: rank.
212. **Couch we**: let us conceal ourselves.

Priest. Her obsequies have been as far enlarg'd
As we have warrantise. Her death was doubtfr :
And, but that great command o'ersways the order,
She should in ground unsanctified have lodg'd
Till the last trumpet; for charitable prayers,   220
Shards, flints, and pebbles, should be thrown on her;
Yet here she is allow'd her virgin crants,
Her maiden strewments, and the bringing home
Of bell and burial.
   Laer. Must there no more be done?
   Priest.   No more be done. 225
We should profane the service of the dead
To sing sage requiem and such rest to her
As to peace-parted souls.
   Laer.   Lay her i' th' earth;
And from her fair and unpolluted flesh
May violets spring! I tell thee, churlish priest.   230
A minist'ring angel shall my sister be
When thou liest howling.
   Ham.   What, the fair Ophelia!
   Queen. Sweets to the sweet; farewell!

                                                      [Scattering flowers.
I hop'd thou shouldst have been my Hamlet's wife;
I thought thy bride-bed to have deck'd, sweet maid,   235
And not have strew'd thy grave.
   Laer.   O, treble woe
Fall ten times treble on that cursed head
Whose wicked deed thy most ingenious sense   ■
Depriv'd thee of! Hold off the earth awhile,
Till I have caught her once more in mine arms.   240
                                            [Leaps into the grave.
Now pile your dust upon the quick and dead,
Till of this flat a mountain you have made
T' o'er-top old Pelion or the skyish head
Of blue Olympus.
   Ham. [*Advancing.*] What is he whose grief
Bears such an emphasis, whose phrase of sorrow   245
Conjures the wand'ring stars, and makes them stand

217. **warrantise**: warranty; authority.
218. **great command**: *i.e.* of the King. **order**: the rule (of the Church).

220. **for**: instead of.
221. **Shards**: pieces of broken pottery.
222. **crants**: a garland or wreath, usually made "of white paper and hung up in the Church on the occasion of a young girl's funeral".
223. **strewments**: flowers strewn on the bier and grave.

227. **sage**: solemn.
228. **peace-parted**: departed in peace.

232. **liest howling**: *i.e.* in hell.

238. **ingenious sense**: quick wits; keen mind.

241. **quick**: alive.

243. **Pelion**: Like **Olympus** (line 244) and **Ossa** (line 273), this was a lofty mountain in Thessaly connected with Classical legend. The Titans, warring against Zeus, piled Pelion on Ossa to get on a level with the gods, who dwelt on Olympus. **skyish**: towering to the sky.
246. **wand'ring stars**: the planets, which wander the sky independently, as opposed to the *fixed stars* which always remain in the same position in relation to each other.

Like wonder-wounded hearers?   This is I,
Hamlet the Dane.   [*Leaps into the grave.*
   Laer.   The devil take thy soul!   [*Grappling with him.*
   Ham.   Thou pray'st not well.
I prithee take thy fingers from my throat;   250
For, though I am not splenitive and rash,
Yet have I in me something dangerous,
Which let thy wiseness fear.   Hold off thy hand.
   King.   Pluck them asunder.
   Queen.   Hamlet! Hamlet!
   All.   Gentlemen!
   Hor.   Good my lord, be quiet.   255
[*The* ATTENDANTS *part them, and they come out of the grave*
   Ham.   Why, I will fight with him upon this theme
Until my eyelids will no longer wag.
   Queen.   O my son, what theme?
   Ham.   I lov'd Ophelia: forty thousand brothers
Could not, with all their quantity of love,   260
Make up my sum.   What wilt thou do for her?
   King.   O, he is mad, Laertes.
   Queen.   For love of God, forbear him.
   Ham.   'S wounds, show me what th' owt do:
Woo't weep, woo't fight, woo't fast, woo't tear thyself,   265
Woo't drink up eisel, eat a crocodile?
I 'll do 't.   Dost come here to whine?
To outface me with leaping in her grave?
Be buried quick with her, and so will I;
And, if thou prate of mountains, let them throw   270
Millions of acres on us, till our ground,
Singeing his pate against the burning zone,
Make Ossa like a wart! Nay, an thou 'lt mouth,
I 'll rant as well as thou.
   Queen.   This is mere madness;
And thus awhile the fit will work on him;   275
Anon, as patient as the female dove
When that her golden couplets are disclos'd,
His silence will sit drooping.
   Ham.   Hear you, sir:

247. **wonder-wounded**: wonder-struck.

251. **splenitive**: easily moved to anger.

257. **wag**: blink.

263. **forbear**: leave him; let him free.

264. **th' owt**: thou wouldst. This is a colloquial form, as **woo't** is for *wouldst thou* in the next line.

266. **eisel**: most editors now agree that this is *vinegar* (see O.E.D. and *Sonnet* CXL, "potions of eisel 'gainst my strong infection"). Gallants of the time performed extravagant feats to prove their love for their mistresses. Such feats included the drinking of nauseous potions.

272. **burning zone**: That area in the heavens through which the sun moves, between the tropics of Capricorn and Cancer.

273. **mouth**: rant.

274. **mere**: pure; sheer.

277. **golden couplets**: The dove lays only two eggs at once, and the young are covered in a golden down, when hatched (**disclos'd**).

What is the reason that you use me thus?
I lov'd you ever.   But it is no matter.   280
Let Hercules himself do what he may,
The cat will mew, and dog will have his day.   [*Exit.*
   King. I pray thee, good Horatio, wait upon him.
                         [*Exit* HORATIO.
[*To* LAERTES.] Strengthen your patience in our last night's
    speech;
We 'll put the matter to the present push.—   285
Good Gertrude, set some watch over your son.—
This grave shall have a living monument
An hour of quiet shortly shall we see;
Till then in patience our proceeding be.   [*Exeunt.*

SCENE II. *Elsinore.   The Castle.*

Enter HAMLET *and* HORATIO.

   Ham. So much for this, sir; now shall you see the other.
You do remember all the circumstance?
   Hor. Remember it, my lord!
   Ham. Sir, in my heart there was a kind of fighting
That would not let me sleep.   Methought I lay   5
Worse than the mutines in the bilboes.   Rashly,
And prais'd be rashness for it—let us know,
Our indiscretion sometime serves us well,
When our deep plots do pall; and that should learn us
There 's a divinity that shapes our ends,   10
Rough-hew them how we will.
   Hor.   That is most certain.
   Ham. Up from my cabin,
My sea-gown scarf'd about me, in the dark
Grop'd I to find out them; had my desire;
Finger'd their packet, and in fine withdrew   15
To mine own room again, making so bold,
My fears forgetting manners, to unseal
Their grand commission; where I found, Horatio,
Ah, royal knavery! an exact command,

282. **dog will have his day**: my turn will come.

285. **present push**: instant trial.

287. **living**: long lasting. Possibly, however, Claudius hints that the living Hamlet's death will supply a memorial to Ophelia.

ACT V.   SCENE II

2. **circumstance**: details.

6. **mutines in the bilboes**: mutineers in fetters.
7. **know**: acknowledge.

9. **pall**: become useless; fail. learn teach

13. **sea-gown**: "a coarse, high-collared, and short-sleeved gown, reaching down to the mid-leg, and used most by seamen and sailors". **scarf'd**: thrown loosely.
15. **Finger'd**: pinched; stole. **in fine**: finally.

19. **exact**: peremptory.

Larded with many several sorts of reasons,   20
Importing Denmark's health and England's too,
With, ho! such bugs and goblins in my life—
That, on the supervise, no leisure bated,
No, not to stay the grinding of the axe,
My head should be struck off.
    Hor.   Is 't possible?   25
    Ham. Here 's the commission; read it at more leisure.
But wilt thou hear now how I did proceed?
    Hor. I beseech you.
    Ham. Being thus benetted round with villainies—
Ere I could make a prologue to my brains,   30
They had begun the play—I sat me down;
Devis'd a new commission; wrote it fair.
I once did hold it, as our statists do,
A baseness to write fair, and labour'd much
How to forget that learning; but, sir, now   35
It did me yeoman's service. Wilt thou know
Th' effect of what I wrote?
    Hor.   Ay, good my lord.
    Ham. An earnest conjuration from the King,
As England was his faithful tributary,
As love between them like the palm might flourish,   40
As peace should still her wheaten garland wear
And stand a comma 'tween their amities,
And many such like as-es of great charge,
That, on the view and knowing of these contents,
Without debatement further more or less,   45
He should those bearers put to sudden death,
Not shriving-time allow'd.
    Hor.   How was this seal'd?
    Ham. Why, even in that was heaven ordinant.
I had my father's signet in my purse,
Which was the model of that Danish seal;   50
Folded the writ up in the form of th' other;
Subscrib'd it, gave 't th' impression, plac'd it safely,
The changeling never known. Now, the next day
Was our sea-fight; and what to this was sequent

20. **Larded with:** full of. **several:** various.

21. **Importing:** concerning.

22. **bugs and goblins:** These seem to be the terrible deeds Hamlet is accused of to justify the execution. Some editors, however, see the line as a parenthesis referring to the treacherous people he is surrounded by, while others read it as the threats against England to ensure that Hamlet is killed. **bugs:** bogies; bugbears.

23. **supervise:** first hasty reading. **bated:** allowed.

30-1. **Ere I could . . . play:** before he could collect himself, a plan was already forming in his mind.

33. **statists:** statesmen.

36. **yeoman's service:** such service as a yeoman may do his superior. Hamlet's good handwriting is a lowly skill, and a yeoman might be expected to serve in a humble way.

41. **wheaten garland:** symbolising prosperity.

42. **stand a comma:** a difficult expression, perhaps best explained by taking *comma* to mean "link" as opposed to a *full stop*.

43. **as-es:** clauses beginning with "as". There is a pun also on *asses* (as was pronounced *ass* in the Midlands), supported by the use of the word **charge,** in two senses, *load and importance.*

48. **ordinant:** directing; controlling.

50. **model:** copy; counterpart.

51. **writ:** writing.

52. **Subscrib'd:** signed.

54. **sequent:** *i.e.* subsequent,

Thou knowest already.   55
    Hor.   So Guildenstern and Rosencrantz go to 't.
    Ham.   Why, man, they did make love to this employment;
They are not near my conscience; their defeat
Does by their own insinuation grow:
'Tis dangerous when the baser nature comes   60
Between the pass and fell incensed points
Of mighty opposites.
    Hor.   Why, what a king is this!
    Ham.   Does it not, think thee, stand me now upon—
He that hath kill'd my king and whor'd my mother;
Popp'd in between th' election and my hopes;   65
Thrown out his angle for my proper life.
And with such coz'nage—is 't not perfect conscience
To quit him with this arm?   And is 't not to be damn'd
To let this canker of our nature come
In further evil?   70
    Hor.   It must be shortly known to him from England
What is the issue of the business there.
    Ham.   It will be short: the interim is mine.
And a man's life 's no more that to say "one".
But I am very sorry, good Horatio,   75
That to Laertes I forgot myself;
For by the image of my cause I see
The portraiture of his.   I 'll court his favours.
But sure the bravery of his grief did put me
Into a tow'ring passion.
    Hor.   Peace; who comes here?   80

Enter young OSRIC.

    Osr.   Your lordship is right welcome back to Denmark.
    Ham.   I humbly thank you, sir.   [*Aside to* HORATIO.]
Dost know this water-fly?
    Hor.   [*Aside to* HAMLET.]   No, my good lord.   84
    Ham.   [*Aside to* HORATIO.]   Thy state is the more gracious;
for 'tis a vice to know him.   He hath much land, and fertile.
Let a beast be lord of beasts, and his crib shall stand at the
king's mess.   'Tis a chough; but, as I say, spacious in the
possession of dirt.

56. **go to 't**: *i.e.* their doom.

58. **defeat**: destruction.
59. **their own insinuation**: their voluntary and sly intervention (in Hamlet's affairs).

61. **pass**: thrust. **fell incensed**: fierce and angry.
62. **opposites**: opponents.

63. **stand me now upon**: rest upon me as a duty to kill Claudius.

65. **th' election**: Dover Wilson points out, with some justification, that it is somewhat late in the play to mention that the Danish throne was elective, and that therefore Shakespeare did not mean his audience to regard it as such. (Lines 342-3 do not help, since *election* may merely mean *choice*, *i.e.* of successor to a throne without an heir.) On this point, see also the note to I. ii. 9.
66. **proper**: own.
67. **coz'nage**: trickery. **perfect conscience**: *i.e.* wholly consistent with a clear conscience.
68. **quit him**: repay him.
69. **canker of our nature**: cancer on humanity.
69-70. **come In**: enter into; indulge in.

77. **cause**: affair; concerns, *i.e.* the loss of a father and perhaps of Ophelia.
79. **bravery**: bravado; ostentation.

83. **water-fly**: a fly which constantly skips up and down on the surface of the water, apparently aimlessly. Osric is therefore insignificant, and idle, yet tries to appear busy.

87-8. **Let a beast . . . mess**: let the most inferior being be rich in herds, and he shall find a place at the King's table.
87. **chough**: jackdaw, and therefore a chatterer.
89. **dirt**: *i.e.* land.

Osr. Sweet lord, if your lordship were at leisure, I should impart a thing to you from his Majesty.   91

Ham. I will receive it, sir, with all diligence of spirit. Put your bonnet to his right use; 'tis for the head.

Osr. I thank your lordship; it is very hot.

Ham. No, believe me, 'tis very cold; the wind is northerly.

Osr. It is indifferent cold, my lord, indeed.   96

Ham. But yet methinks it is very sultry and hot for my complexion.

Osr. Exceedingly, my lord; it is very sultry, as 'twere—I cannot tell how. But, my lord, his Majesty bade me signify to you that 'a has laid a great wager on your head. Sir, this is the matter—   102

Ham. I beseech you, remember.

[HAMLET *moves him to put on his hat.*

Osr. Nay, good my lord; for my ease, in good faith. Sir, here is newly come to court Laertes; believe me, an absolute gentleman, full of most excellent differences, of very soft society and great showing. Indeed, to speak feelingly of him, he is the card or calendar of gentry, for you shall find in him the continent of what part a gentleman would see. 109

Ham. Sir, his definement suffers no perdition in you; though, I know, to divide him inventorially would dozy th' arithmetic of memory, and yet but yaw neither in respect of his quick sail. But, in the verity of extolment, I take him to be a soul of great article, and his infusion of such dearth and rareness, as to make true diction of him, his semblable is his mirror, and who else would trace him, his umbrage, nothing more.   117

Osr. Your lordship speaks most infallibly of him.

Ham. The concernancy, sir? Why do we wrap the gentleman in our more rawer breath?   120

Osr. Sir?

Hor. [*Aside to* HAMLET.] Is 't not possible to understand in another tongue? You will to 't, sir, really.

Ham. What imports the nomination of this gentleman?

Osr. Of Laertes?   125

93. **for the head:** Elizabethans wore their hats indoors. Osric is bareheaded partly out of over-elaborate politeness and affectation. He says he feels hot and is possibly using the hat as a fan. It may have a large plume such as Hamlet makes mocking reference to at III. ii. 263.
96. **indifferent:** fairly; rather.

98. **complexion:** temperament; see note on I. iv. 27.

103. **remember:** *i.e.* remember that you have done enough for courtesy; put on your hat. The full phrase is found in *Love's Labours Lost*, V. i. 103, "I do beseech thee, remember thy courtesy: I beseech thee apparel thy head".
104. **for my ease:** apparently the formal reply in such a case.
105. **absolute:** perfect.
106. **differences:** marks of distinction. **soft:** gentle; polite.
107. **feelingly:** with just discrimination.
108. **card:** map, or compass card. **gentry:** gentility.
109. **continent:** sum total. **what part:** whatever quality.
110. **definement:** description. Hamlet copies Osric's elaborate diction, and baffles him.
111-17. **to divide ... nothing more:** to make an inventory of his qualities would baffle mental arithmetic, and one would reel along trying to catch up with his swift progress in virtues. But to praise him truly, I judge him to be a person of great value, and his innate qualities so precious and rare that, to tell the truth, his likeness is to be found only in his mirror, and whoever else tried to copy him would merely be his shadow, nothing more. **yaw:** deviate from a course, like a ship. **infusion:** qualities infused into him. **dearth:** dearness; costliness. **umbrage:** shadow.

119. **concernancy:** object; point.
120. **rawer:** inferior; commoner.

123. **in another tongue:** *i.e.* in any other language. Horatio wonders at the need for this artificiality of speech. **You will to 't, sir:** "You will manage it (*i.e.* to understand), if you try." Horatio encourages Osric, whose "Sir?" of line 121 indicates that he does not know how to reply.
124. **What imports the nomination:** what is the point of mentioning.
125. **Of Laertes:** Osric is still quite lost.

Hor. [*Aside.*]   His purse is empty already; all 's golden
words are spent.

Ham. Of him, sir.

Osr. I know you are not ignorant—

Ham. I would you did, sir; yet, in faith, if you did, it
would not much approve me. Well, sir.   131

Osr. You are not ignorant of what excellence Laertes is—

Ham. I dare not confess that, lest I should compare with
him in excellence; but to know a man well were to know
himself.   135

Osr. I mean, sir, for his weapon; but in the imputation
laid on him by them, in his meed he 's unfellowed.

Ham. What 's his weapon?

Osr. Rapier and dagger.

Ham. That 's two of his weapons—but well.   140

Osr. The King, sir, hath wager'd with him six Barbary
horses; against the which he has impon'd, as I take it, six
French rapiers and poniards, with their assigns, as girdle,
hangers, and so—three of the carriages, in faith, are very
dear to fancy, very responsive to the hilts, most delicate
carriages, and of very liberal conceit.   146

Ham. What call you the carriages?

Hor. [*Aside to* HAMLET.]   I knew you must be edified by
the margent ere you had done.

Osr. The carriages, sir, are the hangers.   150

Ham. The phrase would be more germane to the matter
if we could carry a cannon by our sides. I would it might
be hangers till then. But on: six Barbary horses against six
French swords, their assigns, and three liberal conceited
carriages; that 's the French bet against the Danish. Why
is this all impon'd, as you call it?   156

Osr. The King, sir, hath laid, sir, that in a dozen passes
between yourself and him he shall not exceed you three hits;
he hath laid on twelve for nine, and it would come to immediate trial if your lordship would vouchsafe the answer. 160

Ham. How if I answer no?

Osr. I mean, my lord, the opposition of your person in
trial.

131. **approve:** commend.   Osric's opinion would be of little value.

134-5. **were to know himself:** one would need to know oneself.
136. **imputation:** reputation.
137. **them, in his meed:** "those in his pay."   Professor P. Alexander points out that the comma is an indication of how the phrase is to be spoken, and not a grammatical separation of "them" from the phrase qualifying it.

142. **impon'd:** staked.
143. **assigns:** what belongs to them; trappings.
144. **hangers:** straps attaching the sword to the belt (*girdle*).   Osric calls them **carriages.**
145. **responsive to:** suited to.
146. **liberal conceit:** elaborate design.

148-9. **by the margent:** by notes in the margin (like modern footnotes). Horatio knew Hamlet would need to have Osric explain his long-winded terms.
151. **germane to the matter:** to the point.

158. **exceed you three hits:** J. Dover Wilson explains that Laertes must win "by at least three up".   Laertes, to counteract the heavy odds, has stipulated that there be twelve bouts instead of the usual nine—"he hath laid on twelve for nine".
160. **answer:** *i.e.* the encounter, as Osric explains in line 162.

Ham.   Sir, I will walk here in the hall.   If it please his
Majesty, it is the breathing time of day with me; let the foils
be brought, the gentleman willing, and the King hold his
purpose, I will win for him an I can; if not, I will gain
nothing but my shame and the odd hits.   168

Osr.   Shall I redeliver you e'en so?

Ham.   To this effect, sir, after what flourish your nature
will.   171

Osr.   I commend my duty to your lordship.

Ham.   Yours, yours.   [*Exit* OSRIC.]   He does well to commend it himself; there are no tongues else for 's turn.   174

Hor.   This lapwing runs away with the shell on his head.

Ham.   'A did comply, sir, with his dug before 'a suck'd it.
Thus has he, and many more of the same bevy, that I know
the drossy age dotes on, only got the tune of the time and
outward habit of encounter—a kind of yesty collection, which
carries them through and through the most fann'd and winnowed opinions; and do but blow them to their trial, the
bubbles are out.   182

Enter a LORD.

Lord.   My lord, his Majesty commended him to you by
young Osric, who brings back to him that you attend him in
the hall.   He sends to know if your pleasure hold to play with
Laertes, or that you will take longer time.   186

Ham.   I am constant to my purposes; they follow the king's
pleasure: if his fitness speaks, mine is ready now—or when-
soever, provided I be so able as now.

Lord.   The King and Queen and all are coming down. 190

Ham.   In happy time.

Lord.   The Queen desires you to use some gentle entertainment to Laertes before you fall to play.

Ham.   She well instructs me.   [*Exit* LORD.

Hor.   You will lose this wager, my lord.   195

Ham.   I do not think so; since he went into France I have
been in continual practice.   I shall win at the odds.   But
thou wouldst not think how ill all 's here about my heart; but
it is no matter.

Hor.   Nay, good my lord—   200

165. **breathing time:** time for exercise.

169. **redeliver you:** return your answer.

173. **yours:** *i.e.* your servant.
174. **no tongues else for 's turn:** no other tongues will commend it.
175. **This lapwing:** the young lapwing was thought to run about with its shell on its head. Young Osric has put on his hat and hurries away as comical and silly as a newly-hatched bird.
176. **comply:** use ceremony.
177. **bevy:** denotes a flock of birds, and probably suggested by *lapwing*.
178. **tune:** jargon.
179. **outward habit of encounter:** superficial manner of address. **yesty:** frothy.
180-2. **through and through . . . out:** Osric's smattering of superficial knowledge enables him to impose upon men with wiser (fann'd and winnowed) opinions; testing him, however, will reveal his emptiness. The image, from brewing, is of a contrast between frothy bubbles of fermentation (Osric's ideas) and barley which has been thoroughly threshed, leaving only good grain and no chaff (*i.e.* sensible opinion). The wind (*i.e.* common sense and experience) will blow the one away, but leaves the other untouched.
184. **attend:** await.

187. **my purposes:** Hamlet intends a double meaning again: (1) to fence, (2) to kill Claudius.

191. **happy time:** good time.
192. **use some gentle entertainment:** act courteously, *i.e.* to apologise for the fight over Ophelia's grave.

197. **continual practice:** he contradicts this at II. ii. 290, but then he was speaking to Rosencrantz and Guildenstern.

Ham. It is but foolery; but it is such a kind of gain-giving
as would perhaps trouble a woman.

Hor. If your mind dislike anything, obey it. I will fore-
stall their repair hither, and say you are not fit.   204

Ham. Not a whit, we defy augury: there is a special providence in the fall of a sparrow. If it be now, 'tis not to
come; if it be not to come, it will be now; if it be not now,
yet it will come—the readiness is all. Since no man owes
of aught he leaves, what is 't to leave betimes? Let be. 209

A table prepared. TRUMPETS, DRUMS, *and* OFFICERS *with
cushions, foils, and daggers. Enter* KING, QUEEN, LAERTES,
and all the STATE.

King. Come, Hamlet, come, and take this hand from me.
                    [*The* KING *puts* LAERTES'S *hand into* HAMLET'S.
Ham. Give me your pardon, sir. I have done you wrong;
But pardon 't, as you are a gentleman.
This presence knows,
And you must needs have heard how I am punish'd
With a sore distraction. What I have done   215
That might your nature, honour, and exception,
Roughly awake, I here proclaim was madness.
Was 't Hamlet wrong'd Laertes? Never Hamlet.
If Hamlet from himself be ta'en away,
And when he 's not himself does wrong Laertes,   220
Then Hamlet does it not, Hamlet denies it.
Who does it, then? His madness. If 't be so,
Hamlet is of the faction that is wrong'd;
His madness is poor Hamlet's enemy.
Sir, in this audience,   225
Let my disclaiming from a purpos'd evil
Free me so far in your most generous thoughts
That I have shot my arrow o'er the house
And hurt my brother.
Laer.   I am satisfied in nature,
Whose motive in this case should stir me most   230
To my revenge; but in my terms of honour
I stand aloof, and will no reconcilement

201. **gain-giving:** misgiving.

205. **augury:** omen; presentiment.

208. **readiness is all:** a sentiment also expressed in *Lear*, V. ii. 9-11, and embodied in several of Shakespeare's tragedies. This speech has been taken as evidence of a fundamental change in Hamlet's character. He is more understanding and mature than he appeared in the first three Acts. (Also, it is only in V. i. that Shakespeare calls our attention to the fact that Hamlet is thirty.) **owes:** owns. The sentence means that since we really own nothing on earth, it does not matter when we leave it.

Stage direction: *A table prepared* probably indicates that the curtains of the inner stage (see Introduction, p. 3) were opened to reveal it. *Foils and daggers* are brought because the duellists will hold a dagger in the left hand to ward off the other's thrusts.

213. **This presence:** *i.e.* those present.

215. **a sore distraction:** Johnson says, "I wish Hamlet had made some other defence; it is unsuitable to the character of a brave or good man to shelter himself in a falsehood". Hamlet does not always act like a gentleman in any case, but the speech is probably meant sincerely enough. He may have "put an antic disposition on", but has been aware of deep mental disturbance in himself, and either believes it was madness, or exaggerates to make the reconciliation as complete as he can.

216. **nature:** feelings. **exception:** disapproval; cp. the phrase "to take exception".

230. **motive:** incitement.

Till by some elder masters of known honour
I have a voice and precedent of peace
To keep my name ungor'd—but till that time   235
I do receive your offer'd love like love,
And will not wrong it.

    Ham.   I embrace it freely;
And will this brother's wager frankly play.
Give us the foils. Come on.

    Laer.   Come, one for me.

    Ham. I 'll be your foil, Laertes; in mine ignorance   240
Your skill shall, like a star i' th' darkest night,
Stick fiery off indeed.

    Laer.   'You mock me, sir.

    Ham. No, by this hand.

    King. Give them the foils, young Osric. Cousin Hamlet,
You know the wager?

    Ham.   Very well, my lord;   245
Your Grace has laid the odds a' th' weaker side.

    King. I do not fear it: I have seen you both;
But since he 's better'd, we have therefore odds.

    Laer. This is too heavy; let me see another.

    Ham. This likes me well. These foils have all a length?

                             [They prepare to play.

    Osr. Ay, my good lord.   251

    King. Set me the stoups of wine upon that table.
If Hamlet give the first or second hit,
Or quit in answer of the third exchange,
Let all the battlements their ordnance fire;   255
The King shall drink to Hamlet's better breath,
And in the cup an union shall he throw,
Richer than that which four successive kings
In Denmark's crown have worn. Give me the cups;
And let the kettle to the trumpet speak,   260
The trumpet to the cannoneer without,
The cannons to the heavens, the heaven to earth,
"Now the King drinks to Hamlet". Come, begin—
And you, the judges, bear a wary eye.

    Ham. Come on, sir.

234-5. a voice . . . ungor'd: an authoritative opinion on and precedents for such a reconciliation, so that my reputation (**name**) is kept unharmed. **ungor'd:** unpierced. Though Laertes personally is ready to forgive, he must, in consideration of his honour, ensure that no one will accuse him of cowardice or any other dishonourable motive, by appealing to wiser judgments. How ironic that with these words of scrupulous attention to honour on his lips, Laertes intends treachery! Like his father, he cares more that he should appear honourable than be so.

240. your foil: your setting, to show you off to best advantage. Hamlet is punning on *foil*, the thin leaf of gold or silver in which a gem was set to show off its brilliance.

242. stick fiery off: stand out brilliantly.

244. young Osric: he is probably in the plot, for he is to judge the contest, and has examined the foils, as he admits in line 251.

248. better'd: improved.

ȝf 1. ⱳuit in answer of: scores a return hit in.

257. union: a pearl of great value. This would be a present to the drinker, *i.e.* Hamlet. While dropping it in, of course, Claudius is also poisoning the wine (and drawing the attention of the audience to the fact).

260. kettle: *i.e.* kettle-drum.

Laer.   Come, my lord.   [*They play.*
Ham.   One.
Laer.   No.
Ham.   Judgment?   265
Osr. A hit, a very palpable hit.
Laer.   Well, again.
King. Stay, give me drink. Hamlet, this pearl is thine;
Here 's to thy health.   [*Drum, trumpets, and shot.*
                    Give him the cup.
Ham. I 'll play this bout first; set it by awhile.
Come.   [*They play.*
Another hit; what say you?
                                             271
Laer. A touch, a touch, I do confess 't.
King. Our son shall win.
Queen. He 's fat, and scant of breath.
Here, Hamlet, take my napkin, rub thy brows.   275
The Queen carouses to thy fortune, Hamlet.
Ham. Good madam!
King.   Gertrude, do not drink.
Queen. I will, my lord; I pray you pardon me.
King. [*Aside.*] It is the poison'd cup; it is too late.
Ham. I dare not drink yet, madam; by and by.   280
Queen. Come, let me wipe thy face.
Laer. My lord, I 'll hit him now.
King.   I do not think 't.
Laer. [*Aside.*] And yet it is almost against my conscience.
Ham. Come, for the third. Laertes, you do but dally;
I pray you pass with your best violence;   285
I am afeard you make a wanton of me.
Laer. Say you so? Come on.   [*They play.*
Osr. Nothing, neither way.
Laer. Have at you now!
                    [LAERTES *wounds* HAMLET: *then, in scuffling,*
                    they change rapiers, and HAMLET *wounds* LAERTES.
King.   Part them; they are incens'd. 289
Ham. Nay, come again.   [*The* QUEEN *falls.*
Osr.   Look to the Queen there, ho!
Hor. They bleed on both sides. How is it, my lord?

274. **fat**: "in poor condition" and so sweating.
275. **napkin**: handkerchief.

282. **now**: *i.e.* in the next bout. As Laertes has lost two bouts, the King despairs of Laertes being able to wound Hamlet.

285. **pass . . . violence**: fence as vigorously as you can.
286. **make a wanton of**: trifle with. Is Laertes's lack of attack due to the knowledge that to hit Hamlet will be an act of murder?

289. **Have at you now**: Laertes's cry suggested that he attacks Hamlet unexpectedly.
Stage direction: *they change rapiers.* Hamlet, being wounded, is now aware of Laertes's treachery, and the exchange is probably deliberate on his part.

Osr. How is 't, Laertes?

Laer. Why, as a woodcock, to mine own springe, Osric;
I am justly kill'd with mine own treachery.   294

Ham. How does the Queen?

King.   She swoons to see them bleed.

Queen. No, no, the drink, the drink! O my dear Hamlet!
The drink, the drink! I am poison'd.   [*Dies.*

Ham. O, villainy! Ho, let the door be lock'd.
Treachery! seek it out.   [LAERTES *falls.*

Laer. It is here, Hamlet. Hamlet, thou art slain;   300
No med'cine in the world can do thee good;
In thee there is not half an hour's life;
The treacherous instrument is in thy hand,
Unbated and envenom'd. The foul practice
Hath turn'd itself on me; lo, here I lie,   305
Never to rise again. Thy mother 's poison'd.
I can no more. The King, the King 's to blame.

Ham. The point envenom'd too!
Then, venom, to thy work.   [*Stabs the* KING.

All. Treason! treason!   310

King. O, yet defend me, friends; I am but hurt.

Ham. Here, thou incestuous, murd'rous, damned Dane,
Drink off this potion. Is thy union here?
Follow my mother.   [KING *dies.*

Laer.   He is justly serv'd:
It is a poison temper'd by himself.   315
Exchange forgiveness with me, noble Hamlet.
Mine and my father's death come not upon thee,
Nor thine on me!   [*Dies.*

Ham. Heaven make thee free of it! I follow thee.
I am dead, Horatio. Wretched queen, adieu!   320
You that look pale and tremble at this chance,
That are but mutes or audience to this act,
Had I but time, as this fell sergeant Death
Is strict in his arrest, O, I could tell you—
But let it be. Horatio, I am dead: 325
Thou livest; report me and my cause aright
To the unsatisfied.

293. **as a woodcock**: woodcocks were trained as decoys for other birds, and sometimes, venturing too near the trap (**springe**), were caught themselves.

304. **Unbated**: unblunted. **practice**: plot

311. **but hurt**: only wounded (*i.e.* not killed).

313. **union**: a quibble on *marriage*. " Is this the end of your marriage to my mother?"

315. **temper'd**: mixed.

322. **mutes**: silent spectators, the word used of actors with no lines to speak.
323. **sergeant**: *i.e.* sherriff's officer.

Hor.   Never believe it.
I am more an antique Roman than a Dane;
Here 's yet some liquor left.
   Ham.   As th' art a man,
Give me the cup. Let go. By heaven, I 'll ha' 't.   330
O God! Horatio, what a wounded name,
Things standing thus unknown, shall live behind me!
If thou didst ever hold me in thy heart,
Absent thee from felicity awhile,
And in this harsh world draw thy breath in pain,   335
To tell my story.   [*March afar off, and shot within.*
           What warlike noise is this?
   Osr. Young Fortinbras, with conquest come from Poland,
To th' ambassadors of England gives
This warlike volley.
   Ham.   O, I die, Horatio!
The potent poison quite o'er-crows my spirit.   340
I cannot live to hear the news from England,
But I do prophesy th' election lights
On Fortinbras; he has my dying voice.
So tell him, with th' occurrents, more and less,   344
Which have solicited—the rest is silence.   [*Dies.*
   Hor. Now cracks a noble heart. Good night, sweet prince,
And flights of angels sing thee to thy rest!   [*March within.*
Why does the drum come hither?

Enter FORTINBRAS *and* ENGLISH AMBASSADORS, *with drum,*
colours, and ATTENDANTS.

   Fort. Where is this sight?
   Hor.   What is it you would see?
If aught of woe or wonder, cease your search.   350
   Fort. This quarry cries on havoc. O proud death,
What feast is toward in thine eternal cell
That thou so many princes at a shot
So bloodily hast struck?
   First Amb.   The sight is dismal;
And our affairs from England come too late: 355
The ears are senseless that should give us hearing

328. **antique Roman:** alluding to the practice of suicide among the Romans. Shakespeare, having just finished *Julius Caesar*, probably had the deaths of Brutus and Cassius in mind.

331. **name:** *i.e.* reputation.
332. **behind:** after.

340. **o'er-crows:** overcomes—a metaphor from cock-fighting.

343. **dying voice:** Hamlet, as rightful king (because Claudius is dead) has a right to nominate a successor.
344. **occurrents, more and less:** events both great and small.
345. **solicited:** prompted (my actions).

351. **quarry cries on havoc:** this heap of slain proclaims indiscriminate slaughter. The words are from hunting, **havoc** being the signal for indiscriminate slaughter.
352. **toward:** being prepared.

To tell him his commandment is fulfill'd,
That Rosencrantz and Guildenstern are dead.
Where should we have our thanks?
   Hor.   Not from his mouth,
Had it th' ability of life to thank you: 360
He never gave commandment for their death.
But since, so jump upon this bloody question,
You from the Polack wars, and you from England,
Are here arrived, give order that these bodies
High on a stage be placed to the view;   365
And let me speak to th' yet unknowing world
How these things came about. So shall you hear
Of carnal, bloody, and unnatural acts;
Of accidental judgments, casual slaughters;
Of deaths put on by cunning and forc'd cause;   370
And, in this upshot, purposes mistook
Fall'n on th' inventors' heads—all this can I
Truly deliver.
   Fort.   Let us haste to hear it,
And call the noblest to the audience.
For me, with sorrow I embrace my fortune;   375
I have some rights of memory in this kingdom,
Which now to claim my vantage doth invite me.
   Hor. Of that I shall have also cause to speak,
And from his mouth whose voice will draw on more.
But let this same be presently perform'd,   380
Even while men's minds are wild, lest more mischance
On plots and errors happen.
   Fort.   Let four captains
Bear Hamlet like a soldier to the stage;
For he was likely, had he been put on,
To have prov'd most royal; and for his passage 385
The soldier's music and the rite of war
Speak loudly for him.
Take up the bodies. Such a sight as this
Becomes the field, but here shows much amiss.
Go, bid the soldiers shoot.   390
            [Exeunt marching. A peal of ordnance shot off.

362. **jump**: exactly; promptly. **question**: affair.

368-72. The events referred to are: in line 368, Claudius's murder of King Hamlet, and marriage to Gertrude; in 369, Hamlet's mistaking Polonius for Claudius, and killing him; in 370, the deaths of Rosencrantz and Guildenstern; in 371-2, the final catastrophe, which killed Laertes and Claudius.

369. **casual**: chance: accidental.

370. **put on**: instigated; prompted.

371. **upshot**: technically the last shot which decided a match in archery.

376. **rights of memory**: rights which are remembered.

379. **draw on more**: bring others to second it.

380. **presently**: immediately.

384. **put on**: *i.e.* on the throne.

385. **passage**: *i.e.* from the world.

389. **Becomes the field**: befits the battlefield.

APPENDIX I

In probable order of composition.

1590. Henry VI, Part ii.
Henry VI, Part iii.
1591. Henry VI, Part i.
1592. Richard III.
Titus Andronicus.
1593. Comedy of Errors.
Two Gentlemen of Verona.
1594. Love's Labour's Lost.
1595. Romeo and Juliet.
Richard II.
1596. Taming of the Shrew.
A Midsummer Night's Dream.
1597. King John.
Merchant of Venice.
Henry IV, Part i.
1598. Henry IV, Part ii.
Merry Wives of Windsor.
1599. Henry V.
Much Ado About Nothing.

1600. As You Like It.
Twelfth Night.
1601. Julius Caesar.
Hamlet.
1602. Troilus and Cressida.
1603. All's Well that Ends Well.
Measure for Measure.
1604. Othello.
1605. *Timon of Athens.*
1606. King Lear.
Macbeth.
1607. Antony and Cleopatra.
Coriolanus.
1608. *Pericles.*
1609. Cymbeline.
1610. The Winter's Tale.
1611. The Tempest.
1612. *Henry VIII.*

Titles in italics are of plays in which it is probable that there is the work of other dramatists besides Shakespeare.

APPENDIX II

General Reference

H. Granville-Barker and G. B. Harrison (eds.), *A Companion to Shakespeare Studies* (London, 1934). Both this and the following book give useful information on the topics discussed in the Introduction to this edition.

F. E. Halliday, *A Shakespeare Companion* (London, 1952).

THE SHAKESPEAREAN THEATRE

C. Walter Hodges, *Shakespeare and the Players* (London, 1948). A short simple account of the playhouses and players, attractively illustrated in colour.

R. Watkins, *Moonlight at the Globe* (London, 1946).

L. Hotson, *Shakespeare's Wooden O* (London, 1959). Dr Hotson argues that Shakespeare's theatre was a "theatre in the round" with the audience on *all* sides of the stage.

THE DEVELOPMENT OF SHAKESPEARE'S STYLE

W. H. Clemen, *The Development of Shakespeare's Imagery* (*English trans.*, London, 1951).

B. Ifor Evans, *The Language of Shakespeare's Plays* (London, 1952).

F. E. Halliday, *Shakespeare and His Critics* (London, 1959), Chap. IV, "The Development of Shakespeare's Style".

DRAMATIC CONVENTIONS

S. L. Bethell, *Shakespeare and the Popular Dramatic Tradition* (London, 1948).

M. C. Bradbrook, *Shakespeare and Elizabethan Poetry* (London, 1951). *Themes and Conventions of Elizabethan Tragedy* (Cambridge, 1935).

H. Fluchère, *Shakespeare* (*trans.*, London, 1953), Section II "Technique".

Hamlet

Shakespeare Survey 9 (Cambridge, 1956). Devoted chiefly to *Hamlet*, this volume has an excellent article by C. Leech on *Hamlet* criticism from 1901-55.

P. Alexander, *Hamlet, Father and Son* (Oxford, 1955). Sees the prince as possessing the virtues of both scholar and soldier. Both courage and humanity are necessary in his situation, and, far from being a failure, he shows himself worthy to be a tragic hero.

S. L. Bethell, *Shakespeare and the Popular Dramatic Tradition* (London, 1948), Chap. 7 (ii) and (iii), on the Player's speech and the Dumb Show.

257

A. C. Bradley, *Shakespearean Tragedy:* Lectures on *Hamlet, Othello, King Lear, Macbeth.* (1904; 2nd ed., 1905). A classic of naturalistic criticism, with both breadth of vision and close attention to detail. Though we may disagree with it in part, we cannot afford to ignore it. Several of the writers listed below are indebted to him, including Charlton, Granville-Barker, and Dover Wilson.

H. B. Charlton, *Shakespearean Tragedy* (Cambridge, 1948).

W. H. Clemen, *The Development of Shakespeare's Imagery* (*English trans.*, London, 1951), Chap. VI. Examines the revelation of Hamlet's character through his speeches—his wide education and the way *things* embody and symbolise thought for him. Notes the imagery of inner corruption.

A. Clutton-Brock, *Shakespeare's Hamlet* (London, 1922).

J. F. Danby, *Shakespeare's Doctrine of Nature* (London, 1949), pp. 146-56. Regards the play as about the confusion between appearance ("seeming") and reality.

T. S. Eliot, *Selected Essays* (London, 1932), pp. 141-7. In an essay which first appeared in *The Sacred Wood* (1920), Eliot regards the play as a failure, with no unity of style. He is influenced by the interpretation of the Freudians.

G. R. Elliott, *Scourge and Minister* (N. Carolina, 1951). Presents Hamlet as unable to act because of conscience, but as he was at first merely revengeful, the delay was justifiable because it allowed him time to achieve an impartial, "just" revenge.

H. C. Goddard, *The Meaning of Shakespeare* (Chicago, 1951). Contains an interesting essay which sees Hamlet as "Jesus asked to be Napoleon". It tends to ignore the brutal side to his character.

H. Granville-Barker, *Prefaces to Shakespeare*, Third Series (London, 1930). An excellent analysis of the play's structure, scene by scene, from a practising dramatist and producer. Rather vague, however, about the central problem of Hamlet's character.

B. Groom, *Essays and Studies by members of the English Association*, XXIV (Oxford, 1939). An article on "The Varieties of Style in *Hamlet*".

G. B. Harrison, *Shakespeare's Tragedies* (London, 1951), Chap. 5. Studies the revenge play elements, but is content to see the play as little more.

A. A. Jack, *Young Hamlet* (London, 1950). Similar in theme to that of G. B. Harrison.

D. G. James, *The Dream of Learning* (Oxford, 1951). Explains the popularity of the play as being based upon its expression of the doubts of a sceptic.

E. Jones, *Hamlet and Oedipus* (London, 1949). A clear and convincing exposition of the Freudian interpretation.

B. Joseph, *Conscience and the King* (London, 1953). Thinks Hamlet doubted the Ghost, and that the theme is a demonstration of how Providence works through chance to achieve divine ends.

G. Wilson Knight, *The Imperial Theme* (London, 1931), Chap. IV. Approaching the plays through their imagery, and seeing them as "extended metaphors", Dr Knight has transformed Shakespearean criticism. This essay sees Hamlet as abnormal and over-sensitive in a superficial but tolerant society. He is evil and destructive as a result of his heart-sickness and his contact with the Ghost.

The Wheel of Fire (Oxford, 1930), Chap. II. Shows that Hamlet as revealed by the imagery is "a sick soul commanded to heal". In contrast, Claudius is an excellent king, forced by Hamlet to commit further crimes. Chap. XV (4th ed., 1949) examines the relevance of the play scene to Hamlet's problems.

L. C. Knights, *Explorations* (London, 1946). Contains an essay on *Prince Hamlet*.

An Approach to Hamlet (London, 1960). Both these interesting works show the influence of Wilson Knight.

J. Lawlor, *The Tragic Sense in Shakespeare* (London, 1960), Chap. II. Hamlet's dilemma is explained as moral scruple, which Shakespeare makes "universal" by making Hamlet unaware of it!

H. Levin, *The Question of Hamlet* (Oxford, 1959). A close analysis of the play, with little new to say, except, perhaps, an interesting analysis of Hamlet's famous soliloquy (III. i) on pp. 69-72.

C. S. Lewis, *The Prince or the Poem* (British Academy Lecture, 1942). A well-argued, lucid examination of *Hamlet* criticism. Hamlet, Professor Lewis maintains, is the representative of all mankind, pondering upon his place in the universe, and on death.

M. M. Mahood, *Shakespeare's Wordplay* (London, 1957), Chap. V. Deals with the significance of the many puns.

M. M. Morozov, *Shakespeare Survey 2* (Cambridge, 1949). An article on "The Individualization of Shakespeare's Characters through Imagery", contains sections on Hamlet, Ophelia, Laertes, Horatio, and Polonius.

K. Muir, *Shakespeare: Hamlet* (London, 1963). A short exposition of the text, clear, balanced, and helpful.

I. Ribner, *Patterns in Shakespearean Tragedy* (London, 1960), Chap. 4. A very clear exposition of the view that Hamlet is an ordinary mortal who learns through his experience the right course to take.

J. M. Robertson, *The Problem of "Hamlet"* (London, 1919). Difficulties in the play are due to the source material, and Shakespeare makes a masterly effort to hint at a psychological solution to the problem of delay, without actually providing one.

A. P. Rossiter, *Angel with Horns* (London, 1961), Chap. 9. Provides a coherent view of the play, with many illuminating comments.

L. L. Schücking, *Character Problems in Shakespeare's Plays* (*English trans.*, New York, 1922). This book is not easily accessible now, but has provided an inspiration for many other critics.

The Meaning of Hamlet (London, 1937). Both these books put the play in its historical setting, the latter giving a useful analysis of Hamlet's character.

R. Speaight, *Nature in Shakespearean Tragedy* (London, 1955). Contains a producer's view, which is a useful corrective to too much scholarly study.

C. F. E. Spurgeon, *Shakespeare's Imagery and What It Tells Us* (Cambridge, 1935), Chap. XV. Deals with the imagery of *Hamlet*, among that of the other tragedies.

E. E. Stoll, *Art and Artifice in Shakespeare* (Cambridge, 1933), Chap. V. Sees no consistency in Hamlet's character, and does not expect psychological realism. The play's power lies in its dramatic effects.

Stratford-upon-Avon Studies *Hamlet* (London, 1963). A volume of essays on various aspects of the play.

E. M. W. Tillyard, *Shakespeare's Problem Plays* (London, 1950), pp. 12-32. Wishes to class the play with the "problem" plays rather than the great tragedies.

A. J. A. Waldock, *Hamlet: A Study in Critical Method* (Cambridge, 1931). Contains a very good summary of the trends of criticism, but brushes aside all problems as irrelevant to theatrical performances.

R. Walker, *The Time is Out of Joint* (London, 1948).

C. C. H. Williamson, *Readings in the Character of Hamlet* (London, 1950).

J. D. Wilson, *What Happens in Hamlet* (Cambridge, 1956). Takes Bradley's view of Hamlet on the whole. Essential to any student, but should be read carefully, for this very detailed and scholarly examination of the play can too easily carry the unwary along with it.